# INSPIRED COLLABORATION

ALA Editions purchases fund advocacy, awareness, and accreditation programs
for library professionals worldwide.

# INSPIRED
# COLLABORATION

IDEAS *for* DISCOVERING *and* APPLYING YOUR POTENTIAL

## DOROTHY STOLTZ

*with* Susan M. Mitchell, Cen Campbell, Rolf Grafwallner,
Kathleen Reif, and Stephanie Mareck Shauck

**ala**
editions

An imprint of the American Library Association
Chicago | 2016

**DOROTHY STOLTZ** coordinates programming and outreach services at Carroll County (MD) Public Library. She spearheaded a successful early literacy training research study, which showed statistically significant increases in early literacy skills of children. With more than thirty years of experience in public libraries, she oversees teamwork, grant writing, programming, community outreach, early literacy training, peer coaching, and mobile services. She writes for professional journals and is coauthor of three previous ALA Editions as well as the ALSC white paper *Media Mentorship in Libraries Serving Youth*. In 2011 she became a member of the PLA/ALSC Every Child Ready to Read Oversight Committee and served as chair for 2014/15. She earned her MLS at Clarion University of Pennsylvania.

---

Extensive effort has gone into ensuring the reliability of the information in this book; however, the publisher makes no warranty, express or implied, with respect to the material contained herein.

ISBNs
978-0-8389-1396-3 (paper)
978-0-8389-1408-3 (PDF)
978-0-8389-1409-0 (ePub)
978-0-8389-1410-6 (Kindle)

**Library of Congress Cataloging-in-Publication Data**
Names: Stoltz, Dorothy, author.
Title: Inspired collaboration : ideas for discovering and applying your potential /
    by Dorothy Stoltz ; with Susan M. Mitchell, Cen Campbell, Rolf Grafwallner, Kathleen Reif,
    Stephanie Mareck Shauck.
Description: Chicago : ALA Editions, an imprint of the American Library Association, 2016. |
    Includes bibliographical references and index.
Identifiers: LCCN 2015036458 | ISBN 9780838913963 (paper)
Subjects: LCSH: Libraries and community. | Library planning. | Community organization. |
    Early childhood education. | Children's libraries—Activity programs. | Libraries and
    community—United States—Case studies.
Classification: LCC Z716.4 .S76 2016 | DDC 021.2—dc23 LC record available at http://lccn.loc
    .gov/2015036458

Cover design by Kimberly Thornton. Images © Markovka/Shutterstock, Inc.
Text design by Alejanda Diaz in the Expo Serif Pro and Interstate typefaces.

♾ This paper meets the requirements of ANSI/NISO Z39.48–1992 (Permanence of Paper).
Printed in the United States of America

20  19  18  17  16      5  4  3  2  1

*In memory of my inspiring mother, Margaret Bobak Stoltz*
~DOROTHY~

*Dedicated to the extraordinary and innovative Judy Center Partnership staff*
*and the families they have served*
~SUSAN~

*To James, my partner in the greatest collaboration of all*
~CEN~

*For Anna*
~ROLF~

*In honor of my mom, Mary Jane Kernan Sanders,*
*the source of my Irish pluck and luck!*
~KATHLEEN~

*For Jake & Sydney*
~STEPHANIE~

# CONTENTS

*Preface* · **ix**
*Acknowledgments* · **xiii**
*Introduction: Let's Celebrate!* · **xv**


## PART I · WHY COLLABORATE?

**1**  The Library's Role ............................................................... 3

**2**  Working Together ............................................................... 9


## PART II · THE TRIALS OF COLLABORATION

**3**  Too Much Red Tape ............................................................ 17

**4**  Striving for Excellence ....................................................... 23

**5**  Gaining Insight ................................................................. 31

**6**  Staying Above the Fray ...................................................... 37

## PART III · A NEW WAY TO PLAN AND IMPLEMENT

**7**  Creating Your Future .......................................................... 47

**8**  Putting Your Principles to Work ........................................... 55

**9**  Avoiding Tales of Woe—or Whoa! ......................................... 61

**10**  Practical Implementation .................................................. 69

## PART IV · ENGAGEMENT—THE HEART OF COLLABORATION

**11**  Growing and Flourishing ................................................... 81

**12**  Sparking Curiosity ............................................................ 87

**13**  Engaging Your Community .................................................. 97

**14**  It's Magic! ....................................................................... 103

**15**  Everyday Efforts, Everyday Greatness ................................ 111

**16**  Inspiring Your Community .................................................. 121

**17**  Celebrating Success! ......................................................... 131

*Afterword* · *141*

*Appendixes* · *143*

   **A**  Worksheet: Growing My Community Collaboration · *145*

   **B**  Using Critical Incidents to Build Leadership Competence · *149*

   **C**  Strategies Inventory: Race to the Top—Early Learning Challenge · *153*

   **D**  Action Plan Sample: Aligned Action Commitments for
Early Childhood Advisory Councils · *155*

   **E**  Colorado Example: Earlier Is Easier · *157*

   **F**  Pondering Everyday Wisdom · *165*

   **G**  ALA Web Extras: Collaboration in Practice · *171*

   **H**  Suggested Reading · *173*

*Index* · *175*

# PREFACE

**Hey pardner, are you ready to journey into a new territory—to expand your** collaborative capabilities and capacity beyond your current thinking? The word *partner* means "joint holder" in old French. In Proto-Germanic, it was *skipam*, meaning "ship or boat." You might say we're all in the same boat—or raft. However, the Proto-Indo-European root for *ship* or *skei* means "to cut or split"—as in cutting through the water. You could also make a case that each "holder" or partner is responsible for cutting or shaping a collaborative effort into a vessel for smooth sailing. We don't want to be ships that pass in the night. We *do* want to run a tight ship to create an effective partnership.

The ultimate partnership is between us (the authors) and the reader—to translate practical programs into your day-to-day library service. Only you the reader can translate our ideas, make them your own, and put them into pragmatic service for your library.

As for this book, Dorothy Stoltz, head of programming and outreach at Carroll County (MD) Public Library, delights in telling how Kathleen Reif, director of St. Mary's County (MD) Library, and Stephanie Shauck, youth services consultant (retired) at the Maryland State Library division, mentored her in the late 1990s to become an early literacy advocate. Putting a fire under Dorothy in Carroll County—and many librarians across Maryland—Kathleen and Stephanie shaped libraries to exemplify the nationally acclaimed Zero to Three's description of the library "as a natural community partner." Dorothy met Susan Mitchell in 2001, when Sue began her post as Carroll County Judy Center director, the school system's early learning prototype. Carroll County's early childhood collaboration won three awards in recent years: Maryland Department of Education Judy Center Statewide Award for Most Improved Partnership (2008), Maryland Department of

Education Judy Center Statewide Award for Innovation (2010), and the National Association of Counties (NACo) Achievement Award for Innovative Programming and Collaboration (2010). They all joined forces with Dr. Rolf Grafwallner, who has led the way in Maryland from his position as assistant state superintendent for a statewide early childhood education priority. Today's new and changing media, such as e-books and apps, offer unprecedented opportunities for early learning if grown-ups use the media as a tool to interact with young children. Cen Campbell, founder of LittleeLit.com, came on board to help our crew navigate the high seas of young children and new media.

Although our collective experience has focused in large part on early childhood initiatives, in this book we offer methods, strategies, and principles of collaboration that can apply to all age groups and aspects of the community.

With a tip of our Stetson to the Backyardigans, let's take a peek at a Texas adventure that can teach us something about collaboration.

Three cowpokes were enjoying a lazy day floating down a river on a raft:

"Three musical instruments are better than one!" Cowboy Joshua exclaimed. "Together we could form a country folk–jazz trio and throw in a little Piedmont blues."

"What a terrific idea!" Cowgirl Amber cheered as she plunked out a tune on her mandolin.

"Hey, it looks like trouble downstream," Cowboy Colton alerted them. They were headed right for a waterfall!

The cowpokes worked together to lasso a tree branch. Then they helped one another climb from the raft to the river bank—but there wasn't time to rescue their instruments.

"Our instruments are lost, but I'm glad you're here, pardners," said Cowboy Joshua.

"We make a laudable team, amigos," Cowboy Colton agreed. "And we can still make it to the Longhorn Saloon for tonight's dance."

At the Longhorn Saloon, the cowpokes discovered their instruments were ready for them on stage. "Our friends must have found them floating in the river and brought them here!" Cowgirl Amber exclaimed.

Joshua, Colton, and Amber picked up their instruments and began to play Nickel Creek's "Elephant in the Corn."

The lesson to be learned in this story is how this group of three cowpokes had to rely on their own skills and courage, lean on each other for help, *and depend on others outside their group*. They ended up playing their musical instruments at the dance because of the help of friends outside their group. Collaborating with other people outside the library to do our best work is what this book is about.

Many libraries are not used to collaborating to the extent necessary to remain relevant for the next three hundred years. As you read, look for the potential within your situation—no matter your starting point—to create a practical yet extraordinary and inspiring collaboration where individuals and families become self-reliant and flourish. To thrive is a community's overarching goal. A library misses its full potential if it does not play a central role in helping a community shine.

# ACKNOWLEDGMENTS

**Dorothy would like to thank the many thoughtful people in and outside** libraries who shared their friendship, experiences, expertise, and time before and during the writing of this book, especially the inspiring staff at Carroll County Public Library and the Local Management Board and all the wonderful collaborators in Maryland, the Association for Library Services to Children, and the Public Library Association. Special thanks to Adreon for your delightful sense of humor.

Susan would like to thank Margaret Williams at Maryland Family Network, Carroll County Early Childhood Consortium members, and Judy Center Partnership staff and our partner families we serve.

Kathleen would like to give special thanks to the many committed and generous library staff whom she has worked with on Public Library Association committees and in Maryland's public libraries, especially the Baltimore County Public Library, the Harford County Library, the Wicomico County Free Library, and the St. Mary's County Library; and Maryland's early childhood professionals who always provided a "seat at the table" for public librarians.

Stephanie would like to express her lasting appreciation for the vision and support of J. Maurice Travillian, Maryland State librarian, and Lillie Dyson, branch chief, Maryland State Department of Education, Division of Library Development and Services in 1998. She remains grateful to the many past and present administrators and youth services librarians and their partners who transformed the public library experience through their willingness to grow along with the children and families.

Thank you to the "new librarian" in all of us, no matter our age, experience, or color of hair.

Special thanks to former Maryland State Superintendent of Schools Nancy S. Grasmick and to former Maryland State Superintendent of Schools Lillian M. Lowery for their vision and enthusiasm for collaborative work.

We like to give a shout-out to Jamie Santoro, a constant source of inspiration, and to all the brilliant folks at ALA Editions.

# INTRODUCTION

## Let's Celebrate!

**For many decades, American families have supported each other. The practice** of neighbors helping neighbors is the genesis of our healthy and burgeoning communities today. The fire department, the post office, and the public library are a few examples of early voluntary associations that continue to strengthen society. These alliances among friends, colleagues, and neighbors put the maxim "Love your neighbor as well as yourself" into action. Neighborly cooperation built communities and fostered individual talents and contributions.

When a barn burned down in the eighteenth or nineteenth century, rural America neighbors showed up the next day with hammers, saws, and wood to rebuild it. "Barn-raising," as it was known, provided required labor. This method of building or rebuilding a barn offered an added opportunity for community socializing. The 1954 movie musical *Seven Brides for Seven Brothers* celebrates the collaborative spirit and depicts this combined work event with eating, courting, dancing . . . and rough-and-tumble fighting between romantic rivals. Helping a neighbor build a barn was approached with the unwritten understanding that this or a similar favor would be returned to any family in need. Or as Tara Kuipers, an educator and facilitator in Wyoming, says in her TEDx talk, "The rule of reciprocity is a fundamental principle in a barn-raising. Community collaboration is like barn-raising. A volunteer fire department is an example of a modern barn-raising. If you are part of an effort to make sure a hungry child has a backpack full of food to take home for the weekend, you are part of a barn-raising."[1]

The spirit of collaboration is a natural force in humanity. This book celebrates that spirit and is designed to help you better understand the value of collaboration.

*Inspired Collaboration* is organized as follows:

**Part One: Why Collaborate?** We answer this question and give tips on cultivating an ideal yet practical perspective.

**Part Two: The Trials of Collaboration.** These include lessons learned, planting seeds, and generating patience and perseverance to help produce positive results.

**Part Three: A New Way to Plan and Implement.** The best place to begin is right here and right now by establishing a core group, starting with clear goals, knowing how to prioritize, distinguishing between good and bad plans, and implementing in practical ways.

**Part Four: Engagement—The Heart of Collaboration.** We'll explore how to best meet challenges, how to spark curiosity to benefit the library and the community, how to engage the community, and what it means to celebrate community.

An array of appendixes offers worksheets and other tools for developing strategies for excellent communication and accountability within your organization as well as among education, business, and other community allies, plus suggested reading. Throughout the text, uncited quotes from those in the field are from interviews by the author or the collaborators in person, on the phone, or by e-mail.

*Inspired Collaboration* is designed for libraries and other community organizations who want to learn to partner more effectively with each other, especially while treading the convoluted pathways of politics, bureaucratic mumbo jumbo, and naysayers. You will be asked to explore "discoveries" about cooperation and collaboration that we uncovered. Questions will be posed at the end of each chapter that are meant to expand your thinking on how to plan for the future of your library and help support individuals and families to be their best—strong and self-reliant. Like Benjamin Franklin's Junto, a group of like-minded aspiring artisans and tradesmen who formed a club for mutual self-improvement to enhance their community, this book is *a celebration of the spirit of collaboration.*

## Note

1. Tara Kuipers, "Community Collaboration Is the Barn-Raising of Our Modern Times," TEDxCody, June 18, 2015, www.youtube.com/watch?v=VH3ZgYmPvAk.

# PART I

# Why Collaborate?

# 1

# THE LIBRARY'S ROLE

*I celebrate myself, and sing myself.*
—WALT WHITMAN

**What is the essence of collaboration? What is the library's role?** What is our best work? It is the ability of library staff to listen and respond to the community. It is the skill of staff—from the circulation clerk to the branch manager to the director—to give time and attention to each person who walks through our doors, physically or virtually. Our best work can be defined as our capacity to genuinely show interest in community folk—whether they are individuals, business owners, or organization representatives—in order to shape our programs and services. How do we start? How do we keep momentum going? How do we grow and change together?

How surprising it is that the very thing that helps us grow and improve as an individual or an organization is often something that we try to avoid. When a colleague doesn't carry his weight on a group project, do you have a conversation with him to address it, or do you avoid it? If you are a shy librarian, do you get busy working with others in order to gain social skills needed to maximize your effectiveness, or do you just accept your silence? Does your department set aside time for reflection—individually and as a group—to ponder what is working well and what is not and needs changing? Have you ever been in a meeting where everything is being discussed *except* Babar the Elephant standing in the middle of the room—whatever issue that might be? Do you create unnecessary red tape in policies and procedures, then avoid tweaking them even when patrons point out why they prevent good customer service? Even though you are aware that gossiping about others never produces positive results, can you stop yourself, or do you continue to indulge in the thrill of gossiping? How do you handle anger, anxiety, guilt, and sarcasm in yourself and others?

A mantra to help us in our collaborative work inside and outside our organizations comes from Stephen Covey, author of *Seven Habits of Highly Effective People*: "Setbacks are inevitable, but misery is a choice."[1] How can we turn stress into something positive and not something to avoid? How can we celebrate ourselves, our colleagues, and our community partners during successes *and* setbacks? How can we harness the energy of adversity and turn it into an advantage?

DISCOVERY #1

## CELEBRATE COLLABORATION!

Let's look at what it means for libraries to celebrate collaboration. Celebrate means "sing praises of" and "practice often." According to the book *Celebrating Life* by Robert Leichtman, MD, and Carl Japikse, many of us ignore celebrating. We tell ourselves that we are too busy, or it's a frivolous activity, or we'll appear to be conceited, or we don't sing praises because we can't carry a tune.

*No matter how busy we are, we should always take time out to celebrate our successes.* The less time we feel we have to spare, the more important it is to find time to praise our work. We can celebrate through song, with food, or simply by pausing to cultivate and experience the joy of our achievement.

Celebrating is *not* an act of arrogance; it is a valuable technique for building a healthy organization or partnership. A daily habit of reviewing and celebrating accomplishments rejuvenates us. Celebrating is not about ignoring issues in life; it's a way to strengthen our ability to meet challenges, harness adversity, solve problems, and listen and respond to the community. As far as carrying a tune, remember that young children don't care if we stay on key during a storytime song, but they intuitively know the value of developing joy in life.

By keeping the focus on the joy of working together for the greater good, a community partnership—no matter how imperfect—can grow and mature to become more effective. Much research has been done on brain development in recent decades to show high levels of activity starting at birth; the key in childhood growth is the development and expansion of thinking skills. In order to develop these skills, young children need to learn how to regulate their behavior, communicate with others, cultivate curiosity about the world, and become master thinkers. Libraries can be a key collaborator—the go-to spot—for parents to discover how to inspire the enjoyment of lifelong learning, nurture "a mind in the making,"[2] and help their children become self-sufficient human beings.

A simple gesture of goodwill and kindness can deeply affect other people. Library staff at all levels and areas of responsibility can attune their radar to attracting people to the library. Once in the library—again, physically or virtually—we have the opportunity to do our best work for communities: to inspire curiosity, demonstrate compassion, and encourage people to think things through in order to learn and contribute to life. We can demonstrate the essence of why a library should collaborate with individuals, families, businesses, and organizations. How can libraries serve young and old, rich and poor, and everyone in between? The answer lies in listening, responding, and celebrating our community's achievements.

Why collaborate? Why not keep it simple and work on our own? Is it worthwhile to take the extra time and effort to collaborate? Yes! Is that extra time well spent?

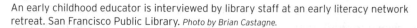

An early childhood educator is interviewed by library staff at an early literacy network retreat. San Francisco Public Library. *Photo by Brian Castagne.*

Yes! As Sakya Pandita, a Buddhist scholar who lived from 1182 to 1251, said, "When many work toward a goal, great things may be accomplished." The collaboration of two or more people or organizations can turn a good service into a great service. If you can handle your mistakes and those of others by tolerating or forgiving them in order to learn and benefit from them, then you have discovered a key to continuous improvement and celebration. What are some practical results of collaborating? Boosting circulation, reaching nonusers, and increasing avenues of financial support are all excellent outcomes of pursuing and celebrating community partnerships.

## Leading the Way to Cooperate and Celebrate

Libraries should excel at cooperation, collaboration, and celebration in order to fulfill our purpose. *The underlying purpose of a library is the enlightenment of humanity in practical ways.* What does this mean? When a father borrows the delightful book *Moo, Baa, La La La!* by Sandra Boynton and reads it to his baby, father and son are strengthening their bond, enjoying the playful and uplifting aspect of life, and learning vocabulary words, such as *snort, snuff,* and *ruff, ruff, ruff.* When a middle school student joins a library teen-advisory board, she is learning teamwork, expressing creative ideas, and helping shape library programs and services. When a wealthy entrepreneur meets with colleagues at the library to discuss projects, he may develop a philanthropic relationship with the library on the one hand; on the other hand, he is bringing the energy of innovation into the community to help solve problems. The library's role is to provide resources and information to engage people to think thoroughly and completely, to enjoy life, and to improve their lives. Libraries can translate this purpose into policies, plans, and the capacity to serve the community.

In the spirit of collaboration with parents and the community, Maryland, as an example, designed an early literacy public library model in 1998 based on the following principles:

- » Parents are their child's first and continuing teacher.
- » Libraries are powerful resources for families.
- » Libraries do their best work for children in collaboration with parents, agencies, and public officials.
- » Information given to parents is based on valid, reliable research.

With a nod to Elizabeth Barrett Browning, let's count the ways to cooperate and celebrate:

I celebrate the depth and breadth and height
My soul can reach, when gaining new insight
Into my neighbor's strengths and ideal grace.
I celebrate the level of every day's
Most quiet need, through joy and sunlight.
I celebrate freely, as we strive for right;
The spirit of unity, I do praise.
I celebrate compassion put to use
In ways that set my thought of beauty ablaze.

At a breakfast gathering in Carroll County, Maryland—to celebrate a boost in school readiness scores—a previously homeless mother spoke in front of seventy-five community members, including elected officials, business people, and parents. She said, "I'm grateful for everyone who has helped me get on my feet again. I'm trying to help a friend of mine in the same way. We support each other so we can be there for our children."[3]

In order to collaborate, a library must first think through the value of doing so. It needs to celebrate the idea of working together. Take a few minutes to ponder the following points and questions.

1. To collaborate means to work and act together for a common purpose or benefit.
2. Why am I a library worker? What purpose do I serve?
3. "People who have good jobs in supportive workplaces are more committed. They're more loyal, they're more likely to stay with their own jobs, they're more likely to give their all to their jobs, to care about their company succeeding," says Galinsky, author of *Mind in the Making*.[4] How do I enrich my library? How do I make the library an uplifting place to work?
4. Why is my position necessary to the service of the library?
5. A colleague wants to attend a meeting of the XYZ community organization to ask what the library can do to support its mission, but she needs me to cover the desk. How do I respond?
6. By keeping the focus on the joy of working together for the greater good, a community partnership—no matter how imperfect—can grow and mature to become more effective. Do I take time to celebrate my individual and partnership's successes, small and large?
7. How can I maintain a sense of celebratory spirit day in and day out, during successes and setbacks, as I collaborate with individuals and groups inside and outside my library organization?

## Notes

1. Stephen Covey, foreword to *The Adversity Advantage* by Paul G. Stoltz and Eric Wei-henmayer (New York: Fireside, 2006), xvii.
2. Ellen Galinsky, *Mind in the Making: The Seven Essential Life Skills Every Child Needs* (New York: William Morrow, 2010).
3. Carroll County Early Childhood Consortium's Celebration Breakfast, April 30, 2013, Westminster, MD.
4. Quoted in Katharine Barrett, "Americans Working Longer," *CNN Money*, April 15, 1998, http://money.cnn.com/1998/04/15/life/working_pkg/index.htm.

# 2

# WORKING TOGETHER

*"Why did you do all this for me?" he asked.*
*"I don't deserve it. I've never done anything for you."*
*"You have been my friend," replied Charlotte. "That in itself is a tremendous thing."*

**—E. B. WHITE, *CHARLOTTE'S WEB***

**Since the ultimate purpose of a library is the enlightenment of** humanity, our common mission with a school system or a church preschool or an agency is expressed through practical and meaningful activities. Are we dedicated to working with teen parents? Can we serve entrepreneurs with a similar—though quieter—enthusiasm used in storytime presentations by our best children's librarians? How can those working in libraries spark curiosity in middle school students, middle-income families, as well as middle-age men—and everyone in between and all around?

"Today's public libraries see serving young children and their caregivers as one of our primary goals," says Marisa Conner, youth services coordinator, Baltimore County (MD) Public Library, "promoting early literacy and a lifelong love of reading and learning, providing parents with the resources they need."

Another example of making "the enlightenment of humanity" an active experience is New York Public Library's experiment with Books at Noon author events in the lobby of their 42nd Street Schwarzman Building. For thirty minutes, Jessica Strand, public programs and events director, asks questions to pull out the best of an author in conversation to a mostly impromptu, standing-room-only crowd.

DISCOVERY #2

## WE HAVE A COMMON MISSION

In Plato's *Apology*, Socrates is characterized as someone who was on a mission (Plato portrayed it as divinely ordained) to expose the specious arrogance of the "wisdom" of Athens' elders. His enemies falsely accused Socrates of corrupting youth—by asking questions and encouraging people to think things through. Public libraries have something in common with this mission: they serve patrons with resources and services to encourage people to think for themselves. Civilization's achievements in literature, music, art, science, and philosophy have developed because individuals and communities have an innate interest in learning and growing.

"Leading the examined life," as Socrates described it, can inspire the library as an organization to cultivate a creative, reliable, and compelling service environment. By examining what works and what doesn't work on a regular basis, a library can tap the strength of an orderly and poised process for decision making. When a library creates a philosophy where each employee is responsible for their own learning, it can connect staff to the library's purpose to support human growth. A library's self-discipline to grow and learn as an organization in order to serve its community magnifies the possibilities and the opportunities to be able to do so.

A school's mission is to provide an education that teaches self-discipline, creativity, and thinking skills—like those Socrates promoted. A public library and a school are natural partners, along with other child-serving agencies. When these entities work together and help a community discover the rules for right collaborations, anything is possible. They create a world full of opportunities for families to become self-reliant and to flourish. They help make extraordinary things happen.

But let's not be piggish. As E. B. White put it in *Charlotte's Web*:

> Said the loud speaker . . . "We should all feel proud and grateful. In the words of the spider's web, ladies and gentlemen, this is some pig." Wilbur blushed. He stood perfectly still and tried to look his best.[1]

## Common Mission Up Close

Margaret Williams is the executive director of an agency dedicated to working with young parents and their children from birth through age three. It was the agency that acted as a training ground for Sue Mitchell, demonstrating best practice strategies to support teen parents while raising their children.

Walking into the conference room, Sue bumps into Margaret, after several years of not seeing each other. Their eyes meet, and immediately they engage in a warm hug. It's the kind of hug that embraces one's soul and expresses deep gratitude.

"How are your boys?" Margaret asks.

"Wonderful," Sue responds. "They are no longer boys but grown men."

"How can that be?" Margaret says with a smile. They nod in understanding about how years of hard work, family time filled with love, and growing and learning as individuals pull them together in this moment.

Sue mentions, "I ran into Jess Dixon just the other day. She graduated a year ago with her master's degree from University of Maryland and is working at an ad agency. She facilitates her own meetings. Her 'baby' is nineteen now, doing well in his first year of college. He plays on the basketball team at school." Without hesitation, Margaret smiles and remembers this young woman as well.

Twenty years earlier, Jess was a teen mom with no support from her family. She was living in a homeless shelter, pregnant at seventeen years old, and angry at the world. Jess's mom had been a teen parent. In an interesting twist of fate, her mother

Inspired and nourished educators gather in a circle to close the annual Early Literacy Buffet. They receive a certificate of professional development, training handouts, and a bag full of new books for classrooms. San Francisco Public Library. *Photo by Brian Castagne.*

threw Jess out of the house when she found out Jess was pregnant, screaming, "You think you would have learned from me how hard it is to raise a child when you don't have any education!"

Jess had no money and no understanding of how she was going to raise a child when she could not take care of herself. And so, she participated in the family-support program Sue was overseeing. The program provided a variety of resources and association of support from many agencies, including the library. The group effort helped Jess overcome the bitterness that she carried around on her shoulders. It took quite a while to engage Jess in a positive upward turn, but when she did, she soared.

When Jess's son was three years old, Sue invited Jess to attend a state meeting to speak with legislators about the challenges of being a teen parent. On the ride home that day, Jess shared, "I'm going to be important and attend meetings like you do one day!"

And now, Jess holds her own meetings and is able to do this because she understands the importance of teamwork.

Sue settles into a chair at the conference and glances over at Margaret. They smile at each other. Sue says, "Thank you for teaching me the importance of cooperation—that building relationships is the key to success for all of us."

## Tips for Healthy Community Collaboration

- » Build on existing relationships.
- » Learn about each other's services and share resources.
- » Plan and implement projects together.
- » Join existing coalitions and networks.
- » Meet with leaders individually and in small groups in informal settings.
- » Invite partners to your internal meetings from time to time.
- » Hold joint trainings and cross-train each other's staff.
- » Market each other's services.
- » Use written agreements as appropriate to clarify communication and create positive expectations.
- » Be proactive in group problem-solving that encourages all partners to benefit.
- » Ask questions of each other to evaluate and improve services.
- » Write collaborative grants and initiate new programs and services in partnership.
- » Be open and expect change.
- » Help each other succeed.[2]

In order to understand a common mission between individuals and among community organizations—and perhaps betwixt pigs and spiders—a library must first think through the value of "working together." Take a few minutes to ponder the following points and questions.

1. How does the library contribute to society?
2. What is the essence of collaboration?
3. List all the possible benefits of pooling resources with community organizations, businesses, and individuals.
4. How can I determine whether a common mission exists between the library and others?
5. How can I harness the power of collaborative work?
6. What part does gratitude play in making the right things happen?

## Notes

1. E. B. White, *Charlotte's Web* (New York: Harper Collins, 2012), 167.
2. Adapted from Sari Feldman and Barbara Jordan, "Together Is Better: The Role of Libraries as Natural Community Partners," *Zero to Three* 21, no. 3 (2001): 30–37.

# PART II

# The Trials
# of Collaboration

# 3

# TOO MUCH RED TAPE

*The disease which inflicts bureaucracy and what they usually die from is routine.*

–JOHN STUART MILL

**A library that does not–from time to time–evaluate its own rules** and layers of supervision is shortsighted. Some people may believe that a shortsighted library or other organization can be an unattractive place to work. Such a workplace often develops a bureaucratic mindset without realizing it.

Who cherishes bureaucracy? Bureaucrats do! A certain kind of bureaucrat sees his or her position as one of having power, prestige, or prominence. They may seem "faceless" and enjoy a confined system of control and tangled organization. Some can–without quite understanding the bigger picture–relish their existence within a world that encourages confusion, struggle, and even negative dialogue.

As a group expands, however, a certain amount of bureaucracy cannot be avoided. An outreach department in a library, an early learning division in a school, the administration of a community bank–all are good examples of small bureaucracies.

If Dorothy, as head of outreach, rarely interacts with a library patron, or if Susan, as director of early learning, has little contact with a student, they can create unnecessary problems for their staff and the people they serve.

# REDUCE BUREAUCRACY

A library director or a superintendent who takes the time to engage in conversations with children and families can reduce the isolation between the "client" and the purpose of an organization.

*Jack-o'-Librarian:* May I experiment with a fall pumpkin painting program where anybody of any age can drop in to paint a pumpkin? We can display them in "pumpkin patches" throughout the library! It will add a bit of pizazz and color to the place.

*Mr. Faceless Bureaucracy:* We can't afford to purchase pumpkins for everyone who would be interested in painting a pumpkin.

*Jack:* Let's promote it as a BYOP—bring your own pumpkin!

*Mr. Bureaucracy:* BYOP will exclude too many families.

*Jack:* I'll ask Kenny's Market and Baugher's Farm to donate pumpkins.

*Mr. Bureaucracy:* All donations must go out for bid to at least nine pumpkin vendors and be voted on and approved by the internal global self-management organizational multigenerational critical-analytical-hypercritical support team.

*Jack:* Wow! I'll have to lower my expectations and put aside my creativity this year. Perhaps I'll forget that I'm a creative person and will become uninterested, unhappy, unconnected, unappealing, and uninspired—like you. (You're my new hero.)

*Mr. Bureaucracy:* No worries, I've got you cowered—I mean, covered. I'll approve that decision.

The art of saying yes! A decorative pumpkin patch successfully on display at the Eldersburg Branch, Carroll County (MD) Public Library.

Bureaucracy grows for a reason, but it needs to be kept small and uncomplicated to allow a library to successfully serve its patrons and fulfill its purpose. Libraries entrenched in Dewey Decimal classifications, "this is how we've always done it" syndrome, and "that's not my job" grumpiness cannot support staff to learn and grow and effectively serve their communities. A school bound by laws and regulations, choked by mandates, and overwhelmed with compliance obligations cannot support teachers to teach children. These barriers to staff success create distrust, apathy, and "I can't wait for retirement" disease.

In professional circles, it is quickly known which organizations tap their staff potential, which envision a bright future, and which provide a sense of purpose—and which do not. Distrust stems from a myriad of impressions. It creates a reef of barriers, which can then be subtly embedded within an organization. One example among heavy-handed, hierarchical bureaucracies is the low fidelity between organizational purpose and what you observe in coworkers around you.

> *Jane Awesome:* I'm doing research for a book I'm writing on pride and prejudice. May I order H. Clarke's *Select Fables of Aesop?* I thought I might find a fable or two to help develop my plot.
>
> *Mr. Faceless Bureaucracy:* (moralistically) "Do not attempt to do too much at once."
>
> *Miss Awesome:* I'm not sure what you mean.
>
> *Mr. Bureaucracy:* "Pride comes before a fall."
>
> *Miss Awesome:* What does that have to do with my request for a book?
>
> *Mr. Bureaucracy:* Well, that just shows that "many a service is met with ingratitude"!
>
> *Miss Awesome:* May I order the book, please?
>
> *Mr. Bureaucracy:* We'll make an exception this one time to provide you with good service, but remember, "you should be content with your lot."

## A Summons for Change

Having a progressive plan that would serve the organization's image, only to be shut down by a superior because it could create too much burden for staff; or creating committees for the pretense of a democratic leadership style while the important decisions are still made among few behind closed doors—situations like these slowly lead to the deterioration of trust and a common vision. In such settings, biding one's time until retirement can seem like a logical escape plan.

Let's first, however, examine how to make the most of the role of work in life and take a fresh look at the retirement option.

» Does retirement become the point of bureaucratic release into a wild, unstructured phase of life?

» Let's turn to the question, what is my role or purpose within my organization?

» How does my work fit into a broader purpose of contributing to society—and serving humanity?

» How can I focus my energy on solving problems and supporting others to develop their best skills?

» How can I develop skills to think—short term and long term—about ways that I can contribute to society and to serve humanity throughout my life?

Our goal in libraries is to create opportunities for individuals and communities to thrive; the place to begin is for library administration and staff to listen and respond to each other. When that doesn't happen, distrust can manifest itself through gossip, blaming others, and cynicism. Resolving such entrenched practices requires a change in leadership's approach to inspire a change of climate within the organization.

## Becoming Less Bureaucratic

"Knowing when to step back and listen helps us transcend challenges and leads to a deeper understanding of our colleagues and project partners," says Katie Campana, doctoral candidate and research assistant for ProjectVIEWS2 at the University of Washington. "ProjectVIEWS2—Valuable Initiatives in Early Learning that Work Successfully, phase two—is a research study measuring early literacy outcomes for children who attend library storytime. As researchers we are not only partnering with librarians from across the state, but we observe the amazing collaborative spirit among those librarians to support and inspire each other to do their best work. We have purposefully minimized bureaucratic red tape, which I think has helped create a pragmatic learning community teaching each other how to step back and listen. The feedback from these storytime presenters to us as researchers and to each other as peers has been instrumental in the success of ProjectVIEWS2."

If a community opens a library system with one paid employee—let's call her Sophie—she will make her own decisions about running the library based on listening and responding to her patrons. She'll consider how and when to purchase books, offer storytimes, or ask for pumpkin donations. Over time, the collection and services grow in demand; the number of staff members grows too. Sophie obtains local funding to hire a circulation clerk and a part-time children's librarian. The library now has a "bureaucracy" because Sophie needs to communicate with her newly hired staff.

The late Dr. Eliza Dresang, Beverly Cleary Professor of Children and Youth Services, University of Washington, headed a three-year study, ProjectVIEWS2, to discover the impact of incorporating early literacy skills in library storytimes.

Although Sophie—as head librarian, library director, commander-in-chief, high admiral, or queen pooh-bah—has the purpose of the organization in mind with each decision she makes, she is responsible for conveying that purpose to staff. Without effective communication up and down the chain of command, confusion prevails. Frontline staff may not understand that the purpose of the library is to help enlighten humanity, which can sometimes best be done by listening and responding to each person who comes into the library to help him or her improve skills and enjoy life. Instead of seeing themselves as servants to boost or sweeten community life, they may believe that the purpose of their work is defined in terms of *personal comfort* as an employee. The result may manifest itself in terms of misguided focus and narrow thinking. The seeds of bureaucracy silently flourish.

Does an employee put unnecessary limits on the number of book checkouts?

Or send the signal to a patron that says "I have more important work to tend to than to serve you"?

Or reduce computer time even when no one is waiting?

Or avoid cheerfulness during a customer transaction?

Or assume that families already know about the storytime schedule?

Or have strict and unrealistic rules in storytime for two-year-olds?

The more layers of delegation within an organization, the more skills a library director or department manager needs in order to convey purpose. By not communicating "purpose" and by not generating effective policies, Sophie has inadvertently put up barriers to delivering outstanding customer service. By reducing bureaucracy, however, and opening up the communication flow, Sophie—or any of us—can transform library service to be its best. The daily interplay between the library patron and Sophie's well-informed staff member is where the rubber meets the road, as they might well say in the best bureaucracy.

One starting point to reduce or minimize bureaucracy can be to challenge everyone to visualize how they see their role fitting into the organization's purpose. For instance, how can one invoke the ideal opportunity for those one intends to serve? It can be said that education—whether it is informal, self-directed education (libraries) or formal, pedagogical learning (schools)—and its role in life have always held a special place for most people. Ralph Waldo Emerson wrote, "The secret of education lies in respecting the pupil." Having the freedom and encouragement to work by this principle—respecting and responding to the student or library patron—could help remove bureaucratic barriers. Developing an internal connection with a library's or school's purpose can help an employee rebuild trust and intrinsic motivation. It can minimize bureaucracy and boost the effectiveness and reputation of an organization. Ellen Riordan, chief of Planning, Programs & Partnerships, Enoch Pratt Free Library, Baltimore, says, "Library rules can sometimes be an obstacle for getting things done. We ask ourselves, what more can we do to support families and help our community partners in their work? That sometimes means loosening up and taking a different approach." In order to understand how to minimize bureaucracy, a library must promote making the right things happen inside and outside the organization.

Take a few minutes to ponder the following points and questions.

1. The "right thing" can be defined as actions—whatever will enrich the purpose of my library, even ten years from now.
2. What is working well in terms of communication and following the library's purpose—that is, what "right things" are already happening in my organization every day?
3. What is missing? How can I help fill in the gaps and make more "right things" happen?
4. How can my library maximize the idea of each staff member "leading from any position"?
5. How can I as a leader tap the power of my organizational structure to make the right things happen?

# 4

# STRIVING FOR EXCELLENCE

*Every moment instructs, and every object: for wisdom is infused into every form.*
—RALPH WALDO EMERSON

**Right things don't magically happen: they require a sense of** right timing, right opportunity, and right cooperation. They emerge or develop from a library's purpose to enlighten humanity. For example, the new Chickasaw Branch of the Orange County Library System in Florida is designed to help enlighten or uplift community members by meeting emerging needs with "coworking" space, a "fab lab" for creativity, dynamic technology-training areas, and outdoor hangout spots. Libraries are providing the capacity for the community to create, think, learn, and improve itself. The community steps up to fulfill its role and desire to learn and grow. What role is played by a library to make options available to an individual, rich or poor, young or old, timid or bold? What role can the individual play in improving his or her opportunities?

DISCOVERY #4

# THINKING THINGS THROUGH

Specific services, collections, and activities vary from neighborhood to neighborhood. An idea or policy or program is "right" because it enriches the library's purpose and serves the individuals in that community. A failure to implement the right idea or activity severely weakens the library.

Every Child Ready to Read @ your library (ECRR), created by the Public Library Association and the Association for Library Services to Children, is like a national treasure chest full of early literacy jewels, baubles, and gemstones. This curriculum or toolkit for librarians is based on research and offers early literacy content for supporting parents in their role as first teacher. ECRR offers ready-to-use video clips demonstrating early literacy practices in action, plus PowerPoint slides and handouts to reinforce content. The beauty of the toolkit can be found in its promotion of five practices: talking, singing, reading, writing, and playing. The strength of ECRR is its flexibility—the only limitation is one's imagination. ECRR can inspire librarians to think about how to better serve and support families through library services.

For example, libraries in Maryland offer "library café discussions" featuring the five practices. "Seventy-seven parents and children showed up at our first library café," says Barbara Graham, youth services coordinator, Wicomico County (MD) Library. "We partnered with the Judy Center, the early learning division at our local school system focused on Title One areas. Many of the families had not been to the library before. All staff were on deck—including our library director, staff, and volunteers—to meet and greet families, guiding them through the evening's activities. Our volunteer coordinator happens to be a culinary arts school graduate and prepared a special array of refreshments. Every Child Ready to Read's five practices were at the heart of our activities. Four activity stations were set up in the library, with one take-home activity: one activity per practice—talk, sing, read, write, and play. Our goal was to create a pleasant experience with the hope that parents would want to come back. We believe we're moving in the right direction because we had several crying children who didn't want to go home."

Wigglers Storytime for birth to twenty-four months in South Kingston (RI) Public Library is successful because it makes the right things happen—active learning through books, music, movement, and play—between librarian and family. Springfield-Greene County (MO) Public Library's signature early literacy program, Racing to Read, reaches out to families one-on-one in the waiting room of the WIC (Women, Infants, and Children) nutritional program office. Nancee Dahms-Stinson, youth services coordinator for Springfield-Greene County library, says, "At-risk families are often focused on immediate, day-to-day concerns. We personalize library service

Baltimore County's early childhood collaboration adopted Every Child Ready to Read @ your library to help parents and caregivers support school readiness. The five early literacy practices adorn the family take-home bag of books and toys. *Photo by Lisa Picker.*

by taking it to families, having conversations about early literacy, reading aloud to their children, and modeling what they can do at home with books and songs and rhyming. It's giving an opportunity for families to personally connect with a librarian. They love it." Columbus (OH) Metropolitan Library created a Ready to Read Corps of early literacy outreach librarians who serve not only families and teen parents, but extend their reach by training home-visiting nurses and low-income housing staff on early literacy.

"No matter the origin of my inspiration—national or local, library or school—the goal is for me to demonstrate and teach parents how to play with their children in ways that help them develop prereading skills," says Claudia Haines, youth services librarian, Homer, Alaska. Librarians encourage families to talk, sing, read, write, and play together. Songs, rhymes, bounces, shakey eggs, board books, and wiggles and giggles are part of the early literacy toolbox.

Other tools for maximizing excellence in libraries include skill development, tenacity, and competence.

## Elaine & Gilda Roadshow

"You already demonstrate and model early literacy practices in your library story-times to great effect," says Elaine Czarnecki, Johns Hopkins University instructor and reading specialist to Maryland children's librarians. "The question is, how can you increase your impact on children? We suggest that you become more intentional about what you are already doing. How can you think about why the components of a storytime are important to children and their development? How can you stretch your focus to not only present storytime but to help parents fulfill their role as first teacher? How can you convey early literacy tips to parents and caregivers during the storytime? The objective is to enhance your role as a librarian who can support parents to inspire their children to learn."[1]

How did an educator like Elaine come to develop close working partnerships with public librarians? A librarian who attended a local reading conference heard Elaine and Dr. Gilda Martinez describe their work as reading specialists at Johns Hopkins University in 1999. They spoke about the importance of parents incorporating public library visits in preschool children's development and school readiness. The librarian told her supervisor, who initiated a meeting between the reading specialists and public library administrators. That meeting led to a training to reinforce early literacy knowledge and storytime presentation techniques, and to develop new skills to interact with parents.

Skills such as thinking things through will increase our power to discern and illuminate our minds. Flexibility, adaptability, and resilience can support our ability to envision, plan, and implement new ideas, as well as reinforce what's working well. Skills such as listening and responding to families help us foresee what public library service can become.

Elaine and Gilda traveled across Maryland in 2000 and 2001 into each of its twenty-four jurisdictions to discuss ideas on how librarians can better model emerging literacy skills, such as oral language comprehension, concepts about print, phonological awareness, and the alphabetic principle. They led discussions about what librarians could do differently to encourage parents and caregivers to extend the storytime at home.

## Mediocrity Is Not an Option

How do you partner with colleagues in your profession when you are being bombarded by a mishmash of visionary forces? On the one hand, you are being asked to envision what public libraries could and should become for children and their families and caregivers. You are also being asked to deal with shorter-range daily issues.

> Your success, satisfaction, and, at times, sanity will rely on your ability to think things through completely.

Influential forces may include leaders in the fields of libraries, education, and health. Early childhood initiatives often have the backing of funders and mandate makers as well as community leaders at the local, state, national, and international levels.

Reading with Sevie. Homer (AK) Public Library.

If your job is to facilitate, navigate, and negotiate between the visionary leaders and frontline staff, stay above the fray of politics, emotional reactions, and mediocrity. Instead, focus on the purpose of the library—to help human beings of all ages think, learn, and enjoy life.

Encouraging a library—or other organization—to create and implement shifts in its processes, staff knowledge, and job requirements creates challenges. It takes tenacity, the ability to stretch your capacity to focus and figure out difficulties.

Imagine weaving a tapestry on a loom. The weaver has "a box of yarns of different colors and weights, a variety of cloth rags, and an assortment of odds and ends, including bits of wire, buttons, twigs, and washers." The librarian has a tenacity toolbox of enthusiasm and patience, and an assortment of competencies, including contemplation, discernment, and right timing.

"Weaving starts with warping the loom frame, choosing and cutting the yarn and making sure it is springy, like wool. Inserting the chopstick and pulling it down to the bottom of the loom creates tension in the warp threads—top to bottom. Pass your ball of weft yarn—side to side—from left to right.

"Don't pull the yarn tight! Make an arc as the yarn goes across the warp threads from left to right. This will leave enough slack so that, as you continue to weave, the tension in the piece will not cause the sides to pull together. With a few more steps and repeating the process—you're weaving"—creating a tapestry![2]

Librarians can use their skills to weave a pattern of excellence into their organizations and collaborations. Don't try to reform the whole organization in one act. Start with one person to build or reestablish a positive relationship, making sure to be flexible and open to growing together. Insert your willingness to connect the library to community needs. Pass your ball of tenacity back and forth, solving problems and creating opportunities to strengthen the collaboration. Don't pull things too tightly—be springy, like wool.

> Librarians can learn tenacity in viewing problems as opportunities that can be nurtured, instead of threats to be avoided.

How does an organization become mediocre and ordinary? A whisper of an idea may pop into your head, or a hint of a solution may come up in a group discussion, but you or the group never explore the idea or solution. Instead, you miss an opportunity to discover something new or to resolve a long-standing problem—you miss the chance to weave a tapestry of excellence.

It may take several years of consistent commitment to excellence to make the right things happen on a broad scale for library staff and their resources and services. But once this commitment is established, staff from administrators to volunteers can use a common language about library purpose, mission, and resources to provide fundamentally altered service to a larger audience than was thought desirable or even possible. By staying above the fray, by rising above mediocrity, library staff become poised to ask the right questions, think maturely, and take reasonable risks. Staff can participate in more decision-making roles both within the library and community due to confidence built on competence and accomplishment.

Ponder the following points and questions about how to think things through.

1. If I am seeking ideas for new services or solutions to challenges, can I use a creative approach, such as Edward de Bono's *Six Thinking Hats*?
2. Feeling good about a plan is not the same as taking steps to follow through and get things done.
3. What does it mean to go above the ordinary?
4. What have I done well lately?
5. Where has my early childhood collaboration or school partnership made progress?
6. What obstacles have I overcome?
7. What similarities does my idea have to baking a cake or playing golf?
8. Where does fear hold me back?
9. What is really important? Where should my focus be?

## Notes

1. Elaine Czarnecki, "It's Never Too Early" (workshop), Hashawa Nature Center, Carroll County, MD, March 2001.
2. Excerpts and information adapted from "Weaving on a Simple Frame Loom," *Hall-Net*, accessed January 2015, http://hallnet.com/Weaving.html; and interviews with weavers Kris Peters, Hanover, PA, and Ann Wisner, Eastern Shore, MD.

# 5

# GAINING INSIGHT

*It does not do to leave a live dragon out of your calculations, if you live near him.*

—J. R. R. TOLKIEN, *THE HOBBIT*

███████ **Planning has an essential role in making the right things happen.** Do libraries plan, however, with any specific end in mind? Do you have planning skills to look ahead and intelligently assess your community's potential five and ten years from now? A skilled librarian starts not with speculation but with an awareness of the essence of an ideal plan, and works from there toward implementation. A plan is worthless unless implemented.

The planning process for some libraries is nothing more than getting excited about an idea—perhaps even inspired by another library or suggestion from a staff member—and brainstorming around how to implement the idea. This process can lead to uninspired services, or to a service that doesn't fit one's community, or to programs that may have an initial success because they are new but do not succeed in the long run.

# CULTIVATE DISCERNMENT

A strong planning process—using discernment—is needed. This process is one that visualizes a plan as a seed that has been planted and will grow into an excellent, proficient reality by carefully thinking it through on several levels. Implementation requires many levels of reflection. Administration can take time to think about the idea germinating into a full-blown service or program meeting the needs of the community. It can invite designated staff to the process and communicate the idea that is up for consideration. This kind of planning should never be confused with brainstorming. The time for a group discussion is after administrators and their staff have invested reflective time on the idea—a week or two weeks or six months, whatever is needed. Group discussion is meant to be a session to help the seed grow and develop. For a lot of organizations and individuals, ideas are a dime a dozen, but proof of mindful planning, successful implementation, and sustained effort and follow-through is rare.

"[Compelling leaders] were all over the map in terms of their personalities, attitudes, values, strengths, and weaknesses. They ranged from extroverted to nearly reclusive, from easygoing to controlling, from generous to parsimonious," wrote Peter Drucker, management consultant, educator, and author, describing people he met during his career. They had, however, several things in common that made them effective:

> They asked, "What needs to be done?"
> They asked, "What is right for the enterprise?"
> They developed action plans.
> They took responsibility for decisions.
> They took responsibility for communicating.
> They were focused on opportunities rather than problems.
> They ran productive meetings.
> They thought and said "we" rather than "I."[1]

This kind of leadership and innovative planning takes discernment—the ability to separate or sift through workable ideas and discard the ones that won't work. Discernment sheds light onto a project, enabling us to see the big picture. It provides a method for understanding the layers of a complex issue. Any tendency to make quick, random decisions for the sake of making a change, or a habit of avoiding change at all costs, will undermine discernment. These tendencies will keep us stuck in superficial ideas and not liberate us to step out of our comfort zones.

The mental skill of discernment involves several competencies, including the courage to question our assumptions, the ability to ask the right questions, the capacity to admit when we are wrong, and an unbiased, honest, and sincere attitude. Discernment works hand in hand with curiosity, compelling us to find what's working and what's not—whether we like it or not. "It isn't what we don't know that gives us trouble, it's what we know that ain't so," as Will Rogers said.

## What Does Discernment Look Like?

How can librarians develop skills of discernment in the planning process? Let's compare the approach taken by two fictitious library directors, Riley of "Paxford Public Library," and Taylor of "Beechworth Library System."

The duty of the director is to separate or sift through workable ideas and discard the ones that won't work. This discernment can be accomplished by reflecting and thinking things through completely. Research is valuable, but only in combination with pondering the underlying purpose of a library—the enlightenment of humanity—its policies, and current community needs. Group discussion enriches the planning process, but only after the director and designated staff nurture an idea and design a preliminary plan of action.

The morning that Riley sets a goal to bring more corporate support to the library, she decides during her commute to the library to hold an impromptu meeting. She asks a large group of staff from all levels to come together for brainstorming right before the library opens. This alarms some staff because they haven't turned on all the public computers yet. It confuses other staff because they expect that their opinion will now be equal to the director's.

Riley hasn't thought about the idea much herself, nor has she told her administrative staff or asked them to ponder it. At the meeting, she plunges in with an exceedingly high level of enthusiasm and charisma: "When I woke up this morning, I'd had an incredible dream. Paxford Public Library boosts its funding for the next hundred years through the generosity of local businesses and companies. As the sun appeared over the horizon, it dawned on me that we have not properly tapped this source for support. Let's brainstorm how we can make this happen!"

Standing next to a flip chart with marker in hand, Riley beams out over the large group crowded into the storytime room. "All ideas will be considered. Let the brainstorming begin!"

One staff member thinks to himself, "Let the stress begin."

Another member sighs to herself, "Let the 'who can be the smartest' show begin."

Administrators, branch managers, information librarians, circulation staff, and others start shouting out the first thoughts that come into their head:

"Let's e-mail all businesses in the area asking for their support."

"I hang out in all the coffeehouses in town. They know who I am. I'll make calls this afternoon telling them we'd like donations for the next one hundred years!"

"Why not ask 'angel investors,' who usually give to start-up businesses, to invest in the library?"

"I do better to write down my ideas. I can create a detailed proposal by tomorrow morning with a hundred ideas for the next hundred years."

"Let's ask one company per day for the next hundred days."

"I like that idea. Why don't we ask each potential funder a hundred questions as to why the library is a good investment. It could be something like this: Why is the library a good investment for *your* company? Let's count the ways! There are one hundred reasons. Number one, the library needs money. Number two, children need the library. Number three, your company likes children, right? Number four . . . well, we can come up with one hundred reasons, I'm sure."

"Sure, we can! And, when they say yes, we can go back with another hundred reasons why they should give a second time to build our coffers beyond our wildest dreams."

"That brings me back to the coffeehouses. They are celebrating 'old-fashioned coffee' week with a free Coffee Roaster & Grinder catalog from a hundred years ago. When I talk with them this afternoon, I can pitch our new corporate sponsorship plan by saying,

"Hey, a hundred years of serving great java will bolster the Paxford Public Library to serve great 'cul-cha.'" Everyone laughs.

Riley thanks everyone and asks her assistant director to draw up an e-mail to go out the next day to potential donors. A few staff stay in the storytime room to brainstorm talking points for the coffeehouse idea so calls can be made that afternoon, as suggested. A few others agree to e-mail back and forth to design the hundred questions to be asked in a sponsor letter. Things are moving quickly. Excitement, nervousness, and dread are in the air.

When Taylor sets a goal to bring more corporate support to the Beechworth Library System, she slowly but steadily takes her organization through a spirited thinking process. She jots down a few brief ideas for herself and sets them aside. She then plants the seed to develop a proficient plan with a select team of senior managers by bringing up the question, how do we use your library branch or outreach department or communications department to secure additional corporate funding? She adds, "As we contact library patrons to find out what the library can do for families, let's ask, what can the library do for you and your business?" Then she drops it for the time being. Meanwhile, managers jot down a few thoughts but put the question onto their "thinking shelf" to germinate.

Howard County (MD) Library System's HiTech students built a hovercraft, which they demonstrate at the HiTech Expo for library and school educators and parents. HiTech is HCLS's STEM education initiative for teens.

Taylor revisits the question six months later. Managers come up with a plan for their unit. With ideas flowing off the thinking shelf, each branch manager writes down how to wine and dine business owners in their service area. They sketch out a special presentation about what their branch can specifically offer businesses in terms of collections, support in technology and social media, and learning activities for their employees. They design a game plan for developing individual relationships and forming partnerships. A key connector will be to invite the business to present a program on a topic of their interest in the library. The outreach manager creates a similar plan to butter up the owners of large child-care centers, schools, and others with a special puppet show for children, plus a readers' theater interactive program for teens. She can tap her relationships with corporate representatives who sit on countywide boards to find out what interests each company. In this way the library will offer program sponsorship opportunities connected to events featuring their interests: history, music, art, author visits, early literacy, STEM, and reading contests. The communication manager comes up with a central system to support corporate fundraising, sponsorship, and grant writing.

The managers—who had planted the seed to develop a plan with their key staff—work with them to think creatively about all the possibilities to answer the director's call to bring more corporate and business support. They will focus on building relationships with corporate partners that will nurture and grow the plan to increase financial support.

As Taylor sits down to review her managers' plans, she is delighted with their ideas to increase corporate donations, ranging from Books and Brew events at the local Irish pub to holding a mini-golf tournament fundraiser inside one of the branches to a classical music evening extravaganza "in the stacks." Fully fleshed-out ideas were turned in for consideration, including how to tap corporate sponsorships for a new innovation lab, an Itty Bitty City play-and-learn room, and using the bookmobile as a tasteful traveling billboard. Other exciting ideas were presented about creating well-timed opportunities for building relationships via chamber of commerce events and invitations to special library activities. An impressive outline is submitted for when and how to contact businesses via letters, e-mails, phone calls, and social media. Taylor appreciates that her primary tenet—what can the library do for you and your business—is a keynote throughout all the planning ideas.

Ponder the following points and questions about discernment.

1. Am I doing what's best for the organization? The community?
2. Do I often choose to take the easy way, or do I take the best way for the organization?
3. Do I consider all possibilities and responsibilities—including the dragon that lives nearby? Does he protect us or threaten us?
4. Am I willing to work with an idea by planting it like a seed to germinate and grow into an excellent, proficient reality?
5. Do I fully consider the consequences—short term and long term—of the choices I make?

### Note

1. Peter F. Drucker, "What Makes an Effective Executive," *Harvard Business Review* (June 2004): 1.

# 6

# STAYING ABOVE
# THE FRAY

*The sign of intelligent people is their ability to control their emotions*
*by the application of reason.*
—MARYA MANNES, AUTHOR AND CRITIC

**In the early childhood field, social and emotional development**
ranks high on the priority list of learning domains or content areas. A kindergart-
ner capable of paying attention to the teacher, following directions, resisting the
temptation to grab a classmate's book or puzzle or iPad, transitioning from one task
to another with ease, and making new friends is more likely to do well in school.
Research has shown that young children who are "ready for school" with basic skills
of self-control and social functioning are more likely to graduate from high school,
get a job, get married, and start a family.[1]

As adults, most of us approach life by striving to develop useful skills, establish
priorities, and work with core values. A value is a principle we cherish, safeguard,
and cultivate. We are willing to invest in our values with our time, effort, and money.
Harry Kraemer, author of *From Values to Action: The Four Principles of Values-Based
Leadership*, writes, "In a values-based organization, people at every level come

together for a higher purpose . . . No matter how productive or financially healthy a company is, without clearly defined values it will have difficulty fostering alignment to tackle problems, surmount challenges, and generate curiosity."[2]

Values are sculpted by the mind and establish a foundation for inner strength—no matter if one's emotions are sad or happy, annoyed or tolerant. If a library considers "love of learning" a core value, each employee embraces the idea of learning anywhere, anytime for him- or herself and for others. Library staff value wisdom and the application of knowledge. It doesn't matter whether someone working in a library happens to be in a good or bad mood on a particular day; the love of learning motivates each person to fulfill the library's underlying purpose to help enlighten humanity through books, information, programs, and services.

The founding of the American republic was based on religious, entrepreneurial, and other deeply seated values, like the love of learning. Thousands of people sold their possessions, paid passage, and risked their lives to sail to New England, Pennsylvania, Maryland, and other colonies to make a fresh start.[3] The learning curve to survive, let alone to thrive, was steep. That's an example of values in action.

We prioritize our goals to help us maximize getting the right things done. We nurture practical skills to carry out our values and more effectively apply the skills in what we think, say, and do. When facing a challenge or correcting a mistake or handling embarrassment, do we stay above the fray or out of the brouhaha in order to be helpful in any given situation? How can we bring out our best skills and talents and those of others to think things through, solve problems, and create new opportunities?

DISCOVERY #6

## ACT WITH SELF-CONTROL

Marie Speck, family therapist, Carroll County (MD) Judy Center Partnership, says, "As we support children as they grow and learn, it's key for adults to model healthy social and emotional interactions with children and each other. We are all—as adults, as human beings—on a learning curve to be our best each day in order to bring out the best in children and the grown-ups in our lives."

Self-control is the "control of one's emotions, desires, or actions by one's own will."[4] "You think yourself a miracle of sensibility; but self-control is what you need," says North Carolina author Mary Boykin Chesnut, writing during the American Civil War. In order to make the right things happen as a community leader in early childhood collaborations or business roundtables, self-control should be practiced a step at a time with each challenging situation. What is the benefit of softening or giving up a stubborn position on how you think a partnership *needs* to move forward? When colleagues tell you that you tend to hog the spotlight, instead of reacting defensively, how can you correct the situation and learn something about yourself?[5]

Deliver the mail and other pretend-play activities in libraries help children develop social and emotional skills. Cecil County (MD) Public Library created Cecil Station Early Learning Centers, based on the Every Child Ready to Read initiative encouraging talking, singing, reading, writing, and playing.

The practice of self-control is linked to establishing priorities and core values. For example, a children's librarian may be motivated to "survive" a day full of morning storytimes and a long afternoon at a Head Start Policy Council meeting. Or she may pause and connect to her core value of growing in the skills to become more effective in her work. In this way she will—despite the extra-busy day—strive to present top-notch storytimes with some of her favorite books in the morning and strengthen her relationships with colleagues and families at Head Start in the afternoon.

Pausing inwardly and stepping back from our emotions can help us shift our attention to our mental capacity for productive decision making. The 2014 report "Humans Optimize Decision Making by Delaying Decision Onset" emphasizes that purposeful attention toward a situation helps develop a proactive response to an issue: "The finding that decision onset can be adjusted to task demands [by pausing mentally] has important implications for the development of training methods to help individuals make [better] decisions."[6]

## What Would Fred Rogers Do?

Fred Rogers—the man behind the *Mister Rogers' Neighborhood* television series—was an educator, minister, and songwriter. He received numerous awards, including a Lifetime Achievement Emmy, and more than forty honorary doctorate degrees in education. He was one of the first to recognize the positive potential of television media for children and set a standard for its use in childhood development.

Junlei Li, PhD, associate professor of Early Learning and Children's Media, Fred Rogers Center, oversees several community initiatives to support educators, trainers, researchers, families, and children in childhood development activities. Throughout these efforts, Li and his students ponder the question "What would Mr. Rogers do?" in addressing present day challenges and opportunities for children's learning and growing. "Whether it is for children or for non-profits having to communicate their causes, [we] think about what Fred would do in his own lifetime then what would we do now . . . We can learn from some of Fred's lessons."

What did Fred Rogers do in his lifetime in regard to supporting the social and emotional growth of children? In one of many examples, Rogers appeared before the United States Senate Subcommittee on Communications. His 1969 testimony was instrumental in securing funds for public television—particularly educational programming for young children, which included *Mister Rogers' Neighborhood* and *Sesame Street*. He emphasized social and emotional education, saying, "If we in public television can only make it clear that feelings are mentionable and manageable, we will have done a great service for mental health." He continued,

> Can I tell you the words of one of [my] songs which I feel are very important . . . This has to do with that good feeling of control which I feel that children need to know is there. And it starts out: "What do you do with the mad that you feel?" And that first line came straight from a child. . . . "What do you do with the mad that you feel when you feel so mad that you could bite? When the whole wide world seems oh so wrong? And nothing you do seems very right. What do you do? . . . Do you pound some clay or some dough? Do you round up friends for a game of tag or see how fast you go? It's great to be able to stop when you've planned a thing that's wrong and be able to do something else instead. And think this song . . . and know that there is something deep inside that helps us become what we can. . . . for a girl can someday be a lady and a boy can someday be a man."[7]

What would Fred Rogers do today to support librarians to do their best to stay above the fray? How can individuals and organizations work together and support each other while treading the convoluted pathways of politics and budget concerns? Rick Fernandes, executive director of the Fred Rogers Center, says, "Fred Rogers was known for his ability to communicate. He emphasized the importance of a caring adult interacting one-on-one with children. He believed that if the television is on at all, adults can help children by co-viewing and carefully selecting what children watch. He worked to find the best ways to create a human connection using technology.

"Fred appreciated who librarians are and what you do for families and children. As you know, he encouraged children to develop skills of self-control to make good decisions. If Fred found something frustrating, he'd find a way to focus on the positive. Fred might do something like clay work or take a long walk in the meadow near his office or play the piano, or he might say that by pausing for a quiet, reflective moment, you can trust that you have the inner 'stuff' to stay above the fray."

The remarkable Fred Rogers of the educational television show *Mister Rogers' Neighborhood*.

© *The Fred Rogers Company. Used with permission.*

Fred Rogers gave an American Library Association conference speech in 1991 that emphasized his love of reading and his endearing relationship with the librarian of the Latrobe (PA) Public Library, fondly referred to as his adopted "Aunt Sara." He said,

I think she knew every book in the place. I know she knew every kid and what we were interested in and what books and magazines had just come in that might need our attention. Aunt Sara McComb was an "appreciator." You could tell she liked books—often by the way she held them. At times it looked like she was even hugging a certain favorite she was about to offer to you. And what's more, you could tell she liked you. Somehow you could just tell. She'd get on the floor with you if you were five, or she'd help you understand some tough word if you were fifteen—and there didn't seem to be any subject that came up that she couldn't suggest some book for. I guess one of the things I remember best about her was the way she'd tell stories about things . . . a picture that she had brought to the library for an indefinite loan . . . or a piece of pottery on her desk . . . or a piece of jewelry that she might wear.

. . . Anyway, I tell you all this because I bring to the work I do for children and their families a great love of books and the people who share them with others. Whether I say it much or not, it's in me; and, if you're acquainted with the kind of children I've been privileged to know, you've discovered that they have a natural way of discerning the truth. The essential truth in being human, as [Antoine de] Saint-Exupéry wrote, "L'essentiel est invisible pour les yeux." What is essential is invisible to the eye.

. . . You are people who give life every day. You enliven and enrich with the tools that our civilization has chosen to preserve and pass on. It's a high calling, and there must be times when it's tough and tiring. I bet Sara McComb got tired many a day, but her love for books and the people who read them carried her through: she never gave up! The number of us human beings who have been touched directly or indirectly by that enthusiastic woman and all the others like her is as countless as the stars on a clear night . . . I applaud your work. I'm grateful for you, and I wish you well in all that you do.[8]

Whether we are dealing with a high-stakes situation like testifying before Congress or making a case for continued funding before the library board, the emotions—ours or those of others—can challenge our ability to stay above the fray. The fray may be office gossip, popularity contests, or a sense of gloom and doom. Brouhaha can be in the form of our own irritations, stubbornness, or a lack of tolerance for the mistakes of others. By focusing our mind to strive to be our best as problem solvers and decision makers, we can stay above the fray. Whether we are offering a new idea for a collaborative project or tapping new sources of funding, a cheerful, sincere, and cooperative approach can keep us above the fray and help us be our best each day.

Take a few minutes to ponder the following points and questions about staying about the fray.

1. How can I become a better listener?
2. When I am in a low mood, what things can turn my mood around?
3. How can I nurture the good in each situation?
4. How can I enrich my work with humor, joy, and harmony?
5. "When I was a boy and I would see scary things in the news, my mother would say to me, "'Look for the helpers. You will always find people who are helping.'" —Fred Rogers[9]

### Notes

1. "Lifetime Effects: The HighScope Perry Preschool Study through Age 40," HighScope, 2005, www.highscope.org/content.asp?contentid=219.
2. Harry M. Kraemer, *From Values to Action: The Four Principles of Values-Based Leadership* (San Francisco: Jossey-Bass, 2011), 7.
3. Read more at "Religion and the Founding of the American Public," Library of Congress, accessed March 2015, http://loc.gov/exhibits/religion/index.html.
4. *The American Heritage Dictionary of the English Language*, 4th ed., s.v. "self-control."
5. Richard Carlson, *The Don't Sweat the Small Stuff Workbook* (New York: MJF Books, 1998), 108–13.

6. Tobias Teichert, Vincent P. Ferrera, and Jack Grinband, "Humans Optimize Decision Making by Delaying Decision Onset" *PLOS ONE* 9, no. 3 (March 2014): 21; see also Richard Feloni, "Why You Should Wait 120 Milliseconds before Making a Decision," *Business Insider*, March 25, 2014, www.businessinsider.com/optimum-decision-making-study-2014-3#ixzz3TAFvBMfq.

7. "Mister Rogers Defending PBS to the US Senate [May 1, 1969]," June 29, 2007, www.youtube.com/watch?v=yXEuEUQIP3Q.

8. Fred M. Rogers, speech at the American Library Association conference, June 30, 1991.

9. Quoted on "Tragic Events," Fred Rogers Company, accessed March 2015, www.fredrogers.org/parents/special-challenges/tragic-events.php.

# PART III

# A New Way to Plan and Implement

# 7

# CREATING YOUR FUTURE

*First, have a definite, clear, practical ideal: a goal, an objective.*
*Second, have the necessary means to achieve your ends:*
*wisdom, money, materials, and methods.*
*Third, adjust all your tools to achieve that end.*

**–ARISTOTLE**

**Can a six-year-old learn the intricacies of Venn diagramming** before learning to add and subtract? Probably yes, but will it help her do better as a fourteen-year-old when she is immersed in algebra? The answer is probably no. An educational math curriculum is an example of a plan in action:

**STEP 1** Learn about numbers, shapes, matching, sorting. (kindergarten)
**STEP 2** Master basic addition and subtraction. (first grade)
**STEP 3** Study intermediate addition and subtraction concepts, along with fractions. (second grade)
**STEP 4** Learn multiplication and basic division. (third grade)
**STEP 5** Work with very large whole numbers; compute the area of a rectangle. (fourth grade)

With a graduated, step-by-step approach, a student in ninth grade will be ready to work with and fully explore linear equations, polynomials, terms, variables—and Venn diagrams.

Scottish-born Andrew Carnegie, an American businessperson in the late nineteenth century, is credited with pioneering a model for philanthropic work. He focused on the idea that money is first to be earned to take care of family needs—spending it sensibly to provide a reasonable level of comfort. The second step is to intelligently give away any excess of money above and beyond those needs: "Surplus wealth is a sacred trust, to be administered during life by its possessor for the best good of his fellow men."[1] His first major charity effort was to develop a step-by-step plan that transformed the American public library into a beacon of societal enlightenment within one generation, from 1889 to 1919.

Carnegie wrote,

> It was from my own early experience that I decided there was no use to which money could be applied so productive of good to boys and girls who have good within them and ability and ambition to develop it, as the founding of a public library in a community which is willing to support it as a municipal institution. I am sure that the future of those libraries I have been privileged to found will prove the correctness of this opinion. For if one boy in each library district, by having access to one of these libraries, is half as much benefited as I was by having access to Colonel Anderson's four hundred well-worn volumes, I shall consider they have not been established in vain.[2]

August Wilson, Pulitzer Prize–winning playwright and American poet, son of an alcoholic white father and an African American mother, grew up in the Hill District, what was then known as "the Harlem of Pittsburgh," in the 1940s and 1950s. His story is an example of how an angry boy on the fringe of society benefited from Carnegie's plan for libraries to nurture the good in people.

Wilson dropped out of tenth grade after a teacher accused him of plagiarizing a paper he wrote on Napoleon I of France. In 1960, at the age of fifteen, Wilson began working menial jobs while using the neighborhood Carnegie Library branch to devour books and educate himself. He said, "It was a huge library. I actually thought they had every book that had been printed. I was able to read anything I wanted. I plotted my own education. I spent five years in the library. To me it was just a wonderful way of doing it. I more or less educated myself."[3]

A smart plan is a step-by-step process that builds on knowledge, increases skills needed for the work at hand, and meets goals and objectives over a period of time. Whether it is studying math to learn logic or spicing up community life by offering library service, the art of planning focuses one's attention in the elements needed.

Smart planning helps the library grow in its ability to serve the community by supporting the joy of learning and contributing to collaborative projects to expand learning opportunities. A lack of planning or shortsighted planning can damage the effectiveness of an organization or partnership and can even lead to its breakdown. The art of planning helps individuals and organizations grow in their mission and vision by implementing goals and objectives.

DISCOVERY #7

## START WITH THE END IN MIND

To produce transformative results, goals need principles. As Stephen Covey, author of the *Seven Habits of Highly Effective People*, says, "Without principles, goals will never have the power to produce quality-of-life results. You can *want* to do the right thing, and you can even want to do it for the right reasons. But if you don't apply the right principles, you can still hit a wall. A principle-based goal is all three: the right thing, for the right reason, in the right way."[4]

Covey lists his second effective habit as "begin with the end in mind." You may have heard this idea called "backward planning," "lesson design," "start at the end," or "connecting with the end in mind." Others have described it as "road-mapping," "reverse engineering," or even "Success starts in the mind, but doesn't end there," "Be clear on your intentions and plans before you start the process," "Steady in, faster out," or "Let the wild rumpus begin!"

This best practice is evidenced in Carnegie's description of starting with his vision and understanding about the benefits of free book lending: "Books which it would have been impossible for me to obtain elsewhere were, by his wise generosity, placed within my reach; and to him [Colonel Anderson] I owe a taste for literature which I would not exchange for all the millions that were ever amassed by man. Life would be quite intolerable without it. Nothing contributed so much to keep my companions and myself clear of low fellowship and bad habits as the beneficence of the good Colonel."[5]

"Begin with the end in mind" is used in the fields of business, technology, education, management, customer service, health, and writing a book, as well as in sports, architecture, philosophy, carpentry, and the culinary arts. "Phrases like 'start with the end in mind' may seem like platitudes but speak to the need for broad changes in how we think—and plan . . . When launched at the beginning of the design process, an operations-focused approach ensures that the enormous capital investment made . . . will produce the most efficient returns possible," says Lee Kirby of Uptime Institute.[6]

*Bits and Pieces Make a Boot*
I'm in pieces, bits and pieces
Nothin' seems to ever go right
I'm in pieces, bits and pieces
'Cause night is day and day is night[7]

This 1964 pop song by the Dave Clark Five reminds us of the importance of the art of planning and starting with the end in mind. One day, a moderately successful merchant—say, in 1650—who sells leather, lace, string, thread, drawknives, hammers, chisels, sewing awls, glue, and other bits and pieces, reflects on how to make his business more successful. He ponders questions such as: What is the purpose of my business? What do I value? What are my talents and those of my children? What is my mission, or how can I contribute to life? What resources can I access—tangible (physical materials, funding) and intangible (patience, determination, friendship)? He thinks back to his studies of Greek philosophy and Aristotle asking himself, what is my goal, what means do I have to achieve it, and how can I adjust my means to be successful? He comes up with a principle-based plan to sell boots and shoes—instead of bits and pieces. Within a month, he and his family hang a new shop sign outside their door that reads: E. B. Sparhawk & Sons Cordwainer.

The public library is an organization of bits and pieces: books, learning activities, staff expertise, and other excellent resources. The idea is to go beyond thinking about these individual pieces and tap the strength of the whole—the purpose of a library in society. This central purpose can be described as activities to help toward the enlightenment of humanity. In this way we are not only helping a storytime mom find new picture books, but supporting her efforts to be her son's first teacher. A thirteen-year-old is not only participating in the Escape the Ordinary summer reading program, but challenging himself to think in new ways to enrich life. We are not so much searching for a copy of *The Boys in the Boat* for the local barbershop owner to enjoy reading about the 1936 Olympic rowing event, as much as helping him explore the concepts of grit, teamwork, and starting with the end in mind.

By helping people, young and old, rich and poor, find resources through their library experience, we are supporting them to explore their interests, solve problems, and develop skills to contribute in life.

## To Plan or Not to Plan

"Planning is an unnatural process; it is much more fun to do something," said English businessman Sir John Harvey-Jones. What does the lack of planning look like in a partnership or collaboration? Let's look at fictional Slippery Run's newly formed early childhood council to make a point. Benjamin, the children's librarian at the village library, invites representatives from the local school, social services, a bank, a general store, a child-care center, and a church preschool, plus a stay-at-home mom, a mom who uses the child-care center, and a representative from the mayor's office for a discussion about supporting families with young children. The group sits down for their first formal meeting. Benjamin starts the discussion by saying, "Thank you for coming today. I've asked you here to help figure out what we can do to turn around our dismal high school graduation statistics. But focusing on our high school students only contravenes much of what research says about prevention. We need to start earlier! Much earlier!"

"Speaking on behalf of the schools, we think it's a good idea to start earlier."
"We can donate $10,000 toward the cause!"
"Children need to know how to spell their name before they go to school."
"My store has a twenty-dollar Learn-to-Spell-Your-Name Kit for four-year-olds."
"We can purchase five hundred of the kits. Although we have only fifty four-year-olds in the village, it means that we'll have a ten-year supply."
"I can help distribute the kits each year to my mom's group."

Picture-book time at Pierce County (WA) Library System. *Photo by Chris Tumbusch.*

"We'll post the initiative on the village website."

"Wow! We've created a trajectory of success for the village for years to come!"

Of course, ten years later, the high school graduation statistics have not improved. Although most children know how to spell their name upon entering kindergarten, many do not have exposure to storybooks and poems, nor can they recognize rhyming words in spoken language. Many others are unable to demonstrate age-appropriate decision making or play with others cooperatively, or even show the ability to resolve conflicts.

Although this scenario is over the top, it demonstrates how easy it is to get swept away in the wrong direction. Benjamin successfully gathered a broad-based group of stakeholders to the community table, but neither he nor anyone else was willing to step up to take the lead in defining the group's purpose. No one asked key questions, such as, what is our purpose, what does the group value, what are our goals, what means do we have to achieve them, and how can we adjust our means to be successful? Instead, the group focused on one tiny bit—children learning to spell their names—to support families as they inspire their children to learn. What he lacked was a plan.

"No millionaire will go far wrong in his search for one of the best forms for the use of his surplus who chooses to establish a free library in any community that is willing to maintain and develop it," wrote Andrew Carnegie in an article that first appeared in the *North American Review* in 1889.[8] Carnegie funded 2,589 libraries around the globe, starting with a library in his hometown of Dunfermline, Scotland, in 1881. By the early 1920s, 1,681 Carnegie libraries were constructed in the United States.[9] What was his plan that reinvented the American public library?

Carnegie established a simple yet effective grant framework. These grants bolstered the public library by creating partnerships with community leaders to encourage and support lifelong learning. Carnegie gave a large donation but required towns to provide a portion of the costs as well as ongoing expenses to keep the library operational. In addition, the grant directed libraries to offer free service and guided librarians to interact with and better serve patrons by requiring open stacks and effective dialogue about reading interests.[10]

In the early part of the twenty-first century, the number and use of public libraries—Carnegie-funded or otherwise—is astounding. There are nearly 9,000 public libraries with approximately 17,000 individual public library outlets in the fifty states, the District of Columbia, and outlying territories.[11] There were 1.5 billion in-person visits to public libraries across the United States in fiscal year 2012. This was a ten-year increase of more than 20 percent. More than 2.2 billion books and materials were circulated in public libraries, a ten-year increase of 28 percent. More than 92 million people attended the four million programs at public libraries.[12]

Without an effective, coherent plan, any initiative is doomed to fall short of its goal. We don't start with a plea for more money and then figure out how to spend it. We must refuse to plunge into these kinds of poor planning techniques. Instead we persevere and, like Andrew Carnegie, ask the right questions to develop useful skills and habits for the art of planning. We can ally ourselves with the skill of starting with the end in mind.

Questions to ponder about the art of planning:

1. What is the purpose of the library? What is the purpose of my unit within the library?
2. What is my role within the organization? How can I enrich the library's purpose?
3. What is the purpose of this collaboration? What is the purpose of the library within the collaboration?
4. What is my role within the collaboration? How can I enrich the collaboration's purpose?
5. How can I be proactive? Do I see that mental creations precede my actions?
6. What goals can I set to transform my values and skills into specific projects?
7. How can I start with the end in mind to specifically support a collaborative effort?

## Notes

1. Burton J., Hendrick, ed., *Miscellaneous Writings of Andrew Carnegie*, vol. 2 (New York: Doubleday, Doran, 1933), 206.
2. Andrew Carnegie, *Autobiography of Andrew Carnegie* (Boston: Houghton Mifflin, 1920), 45.
3. "The August Wilson Education Project: Timeline," WQED, accessed March 2015, www.wqed.org/augustwilson/timeline.
4. Stephen R. Covey, A. Roger Merrill, and Rebecca R. Merrill, *First Things First: To Live, to Love, to Learn, to Leave a Legacy* (New York: Simon & Schuster, 1994), 146.
5. Carnegie, *Autobiography*, 44–45.
6. Lee Kirby, "Start with the End in Mind!" Uptime Institute, accessed March 2015, http://journal.uptimeinstitute.com/best-practice-is-to-start-with-the-end-in-mind/.
7. Dave Clark and Michael George Smith, "Bits and Pieces," 1964, accessed March 2015, www.metrolyrics.com/bits-and-pieces-lyrics-dave-clark-five.html.
8. Andrew Carnegie, *The Gospel of Wealth* (1901; Atlanta: Kudzu House, 2008), 71–72.
9. Joseph Frazier Wall, *Andrew Carnegie* (Pittsburgh, PA: University of Pittsburgh Press, 1989), 1101.

10. Adapted from Dorothy Stoltz, Marisa Conner, and James Bradberry, *The Power of Play: Designing Early Learning Spaces* (Chicago: ALA Editions, 2015), 17.

11. Institute of Museum of Library Services, "Public Libraries in the United States Survey," accessed March 2015, www.imls.gov/research/public_libraries_in_the_united_states_survey.aspx.

12. Institute of Museum of Library Services, "Public Libraries in the United States Survey, FY 2012, Fast Facts Report," 2012, www.imls.gov/assets/1/AssetManager/Fast_Facts_PLS_FY2012.pdf.

# 8

# PUTTING YOUR PRINCIPLES TO WORK

*The key is not to prioritize what's on your schedule, but to schedule your priorities.*
**–STEPHEN COVEY, AUTHOR, EDUCATOR, BUSINESSMAN**

**Benjamin Franklin—writer, inventor, scientist, polymath, and** "first citizen of eighteenth-century America"—started his day with the question, "What good shall I do this day?" He ended the day with, "What good have I done today?" In 1730, he contemplated the need for a public library. This first Philadelphia library was not free, but it was open to the public, that is, to those who could afford to pay a subscription.

"Those who loved reading were obliged to send for their books from England; the members of the Junto [a group of like-minded aspiring artisans and tradesmen focused on self- improvement to enhance their community] had each a few," Franklin wrote in his autobiography. He suggested that each person bring their private library of books to a rented room for members to borrow. Soon the small makeshift library collection was insufficient for the group's insatiable reading interests.

He continued, "Finding the advantage of this collection, I proposed to render the benefit from books more common, by commencing a public subscription library [to encourage others to join the book exchange beyond the Junto members]." He sketched a plan and created rules that included a registration fee and annual library membership dues from subscribers. Few people were readers at that time or had much money, but it was a start. The library "company" was open one day a week and soon proved its value. Other towns imitated this new institution. Franklin observed that reading became "fashionable and our people, having no public amusements to divert their attention from study, became better acquainted with books, and in a few years were observed by strangers to be better instructed and more intelligent than people of the same rank generally are in other countries."[1]

DISCOVERY # 8

# CHUNK IT DOWN

Planning and making choices may be challenging, but it can be done. Thinking things through along with careful decision making forces you to identify your criteria in prioritizing. "In most cases, unless four or five strategically consequential 'chunks of work' are defined and approached, the organization may never achieve much of its vision at all," says Alain Gauthier, Core Leadership Development.[2]

Franklin applied this method—of prioritizing and breaking the work down into manageable bits—to his idea of a lending library for his Junto or practical philosophy club. The original goal was to discuss ideas and share books for mutual improvement. The first meetings were held at a local alehouse. The establishment of a library of

Books & Bars with moderator Jeff Kamin, cosponsored by the Friends of the Saint Paul (MN) Library, takes the standard book club to the local pub.

books and the expansion of that collection became top priorities to increase the group's effectiveness. Franklin chunked down the process of how to work with these priorities. His to-do list might have looked like this:

» Establish goals based on thoughtful principles of living—doing the right thing, for the right reason, in the right way.
» Locate a room to rent outside the pub for a quieter atmosphere for discussion and to store the books.
» Sketch out a plan for the purchase and lending of books with conveyancer Mr. Charles Brockden, establishing a "library company."
» Dismiss—respectfully—Mr. Brockden's concerns that subscribers signing up for fifty years will all be dead when their membership expires.
» Trust your hunch that this is the right thing for the right reason. (In fact, Franklin and several original members remained living at the time the subscription expired. Within a few years after the library company was established, however, the charter gave perpetuity to the company.)
» Develop a strategy to solicit subscriptions beyond Junto members. (Franklin found that presenting the library idea as his idea rubbed people the wrong way. He explains his method: "I put myself as much as I could out of sight, and stated it as a scheme of *a number of friends,* who had requested me to go about and propose it to such as they thought lovers of reading. In this way my affair went on more smoothly, and I ever practiced it on such occasions; and, from my frequent successes, can heartily recommend it."[3])

## What Would Benjamin Franklin Do?

"Franklin picked up his penchant for forming do-good associations . . . [and community organizations, such as the lending library, fire brigade, and the hospital], but his organizational fervor and galvanizing personality made him the most influential force in instilling this as an enduring part of American life," writes historian Walter Isaacson. The extraordinary weaving together of individualistic and community-based approaches to living was central to Franklin and the American community he was helping to create. "The frontier attracted barn-raising pioneers who were ruggedly individualistic as well as fiercely supportive of their community. Franklin was the epitome of this admixture of self-reliance and civic involvement, and what he exemplified became part of the American character."[4]

What would Ben Franklin do today to support librarians to do their best to prioritize their work and develop community collaborations? The aged sage might pen a letter such as this:

Dear Librarian,

I am charmed with your popular "strategic planning" concepts for the library of today, and your ability to change with the times; and I approve much of your conclusion that we should draw all the good we can from this world. In my opinion, we might all draw more good from it than we do if we take care not to give too much for *whistles*. For me it seems that most of the struggling libraries and communities become so by neglect of that caution.

You ask what I mean? When I was a child, I was charmed with the sound of a whistle; and in a hurried, nonthinking manner, gave all my money for one in a rushed negotiation with another boy. I then went whistling all over the house, much pleased with my whistle but disturbing my entire family. My brothers and sisters told me I had given four times as much as it was worth; put me in mind what good things I might have bought with the rest of the money; and laughed at me so much for my folly, that I cried with vexation; and the reflection gave me more chagrin than the whistle gave me pleasure.

This, however, was afterward of use to me, the impression continuing on my mind; so that often, when I was tempted to buy some unnecessary thing, I said to myself, *Don't give too much for the whistle*, and I saved my money.

As I look around the library world, and observe the organizational and collaborative planning in recent years, I think I meet with many who give too much for the whistle.

When I see someone too ambitious of political favor, sacrificing his time in attendance of myriad town meetings, his repose, his independence, his core values, and perhaps his friends, to attain it, in the name of the library mission, I say to myself, *This library director gives too much for his whistle.*

If I see a librarian buy many, very many, books, but none of Plato and Socrates or no biographies of Leonardo da Vinci or me, *Poor lass,* say I, *you pay too much for your whistle.*

When I know a miser who gave up every kind of quality purchase of books, technology, and furniture, all the pleasure of doing good for others and offering excellent service delivery, all the esteem of his colleagues, and the joys of benevolent friendship, for the sake of accumulating wealth, *Alas!* says I, *You pay too much for your whistle.*

If I see one fond of appearance and a staid environment above quality customer service, preventing a patron from feeling welcome as they enter the library, or upsetting a child because too many educational toys are out of their bins in the play and learn center, *What a pity,* say I, *that he should pay so much for a whistle.*

When I meet a librarian who is distracted and grumpy when I go up to the service desk, missing a golden opportunity to ask what more can the library do for you, *She pays*, indeed, say I, *too much for her whistle.*

In short, I conceive that a great part of the problems of librarians are brought upon them by the false estimates they have made of the value of things, and by their giving too much for their whistles.

Yet with all this wisdom of which I am boasting, there are certain things in this world so tempting—for example, the apples on my backyard tree when perfectly ripe—which happily are not to be bought; for if they were to be put to sale by auction, I might very easily be led to ruin myself in the purchase, and find myself once more given too much for the whistle.

Adieu, my dear friend, my public librarian, and believe me ever yours very sincerely and with unalterable affection,

—*B. Franklin*[5]

Take a few minutes to ponder the following points and questions about prioritizing and chunking things down.

1. How can I establish goals based on thoughtful principles of living—doing the right thing, for the right reason, in the right way?
2. What top two or three priorities should our collaborative project focus on this year? How do I think things through for each priority and chunk it down by tasks involved to reach our goal?
3. What good can I do today? What good have I done today?
4. How do I stay focused on top priorities and avoid spending too much for my "whistle"?
5. Ponder the motto of the Library Company of Philadelphia, written by Benjamin Franklin: *Communiter Bona profundere Deum est* (To pour forth benefits for the common good is divine).

### Notes

1. Peter Shaw, ed., *The Autobiography and Other Writings by Benjamin Franklin* (New York: Bantam Books, 1982), 71–72.
2. Core Leadership Development, http://alaingauthier.org/.
3. Shaw, *Writings by Benjamin Franklin*, 72.
4. Walter Isaacson, *Benjamin Franklin: An American Life* (New York: Simon & Schuster, 2003), 102–03.
5. Adapted from Shaw, *Writings by Benjamin Franklin*, 256–58.

# 9

# AVOIDING TALES OF
# WOE-OR WHOA!

*Let the future tell the truth, and evaluate each one*
*according to his work and accomplishments.*
**—NIKOLA TESLA, ELECTRICAL ENGINEER, INVENTOR, PHYSICIST, FUTURIST**

Let the day be forever remember'd with pride
That beheld the proud Hudson to Erie allied
O the last sand of Time from his glass shall descend
Ere a union, so fruitful of glory shall end
Ere a union, so fruitful of glory shall end[1]

When was the last time you rode the Erie Canal? We never have! Not only was it replaced by the railroad, but the railroad was also replaced by the New York State Thruway. "While some of the public was wary of railroads at first such as claiming them to be a 'device of the devil' as one school board in Ohio put it or that travel by train would cause a 'concussion of the brain,' the efficiency they brought could not be argued. For instance, railroads could cut the distant it took between cities by steamboat in half. A good example is traveling between Cincinnati and St. Louis.

By water this trip took 702 miles and three days but by railroad it took only 339 miles and 16 hours."[2]

Whether it's in a railroad company, library, business, church, or government, if centralized theorists create a plan without being in touch with frontline services or sales, it's more than likely to be a bad plan. A bad plan is one that isn't thought through and produces an ineffective collaboration and poor results. Does a plan have goals that can lead to something you like, or are the goals not carefully considered, likely to lead to consequences you don't anticipate? To avoid a bad plan, think about potential consequences.

During the Soviet Union's first five-year plan, expectations were extraordinarily high from the central office: a 110 percent increase in coal production, 200 percent in iron production, 335 percent in electric power, and 70 percent in wages.[3] Ella Winter, an Australian-British journalist and activist, visited the Soviet Union in 1931 and found it struggling to modernize. She described excitement in the new changes and vision, but also "an inefficiency that could drive one to desperation." She surmised in an essay that the changes were so rapid and most people had little experience in the new jobs, "and centuries of apathy to overcome, and perhaps . . . they can get jobs whether they're [the jobs are] good or not. But it takes days to get anything done. They never make an appointment, they tell you to come and then they'll arrange when you must telephone again to ask for an appointment. Lifts are always out of order; a current anecdote has a 'lift factory' entirely devoted to manufacture of the notices LIFT OUT OF ORDER."[4]

We need to make sure that libraries are never posted as out of order. Planning is the key.

DISCOVERY # 9

## DISTINGUISH BETWEEN GOOD PLANS AND BAD ONES

Is your library becoming obsolete? Does the book-of-the-month club do more for literacy needs and literary enthusiasm than a library? We say no, it does not! However, is a library needed in every community? Before jumping to your department of gloom and doom, ponder this for a moment: this question is disheartening only if you try to answer it in terms of the past. If you look to the future, the answers take on a vibrant, consistent, and exciting spirit.

Although libraries have been destroyed, like the Library of Alexandria in ancient times, or closed, like some libraries in both heavily populated and rural areas in recent years, many more libraries have not only stayed open but are transforming themselves to bequeath collections, core values, and community culture to future generations. Reaching out to families with young children and supporting the parent as first teacher is one potential example of a good plan to transform libraries. Other examples, depending on your local community, could be to find new connections with local businesses, youth, and creative adults. A bad plan is one that does not divorce itself from the past. Let's plan not from what has been, but from what might be.

Discovery #9 helps us ask the right questions around the future of the library and its role in community collaborations. A successful library of the future is one in pursuit of identity. What is the real goal—and glory—of a library? If the answer is to help support the enlightenment of humanity by offering practical programs and services, then let's get busy keeping libraries alive. Let us plan how to animate this "do-good association" to help a community thrive. In large part, Franklin and Carnegie's basic literacy goal has been achieved in the United States. We're not saying that portions of our communities do not have literacy problems. Most people, however, know how to read well enough to take advantage of opportunities to nurture their hearts, mind, and soul through reading books, articles, and ponderings in all formats.

The opportunity to enrich and improve oneself in order to support the betterment of society was a larger goal of Franklin and Carnegie. Are libraries today focused on this larger goal?

Let's first explore this question: What are libraries doing today that might lead to extinction?

» Does your library provide poor customer service?
» Is it stuck in the past?
» Do staff members have an aversion to new and emerging technologies?
» Is there little or no thought behind collection development in terms of bequeathing it to future generations?
» Are staff members scheduled in a way to prevent attendance at a chamber of commerce or early childhood–focused community meeting?

Depending on the community, a library may take on a social work–like focus, but we are not social services. A library may take on a formal education-like focus, but we are not a school or college. In a collaborative effort, the library—in its role to help enlighten humanity—has the right focus to support our schools and social work agencies in their missions. Here's the key to our future: we offer something beyond anyone else's capabilities.

Some would say the library's future role is to inspire individuals of all ages to explore their interests in life:

What about the eighth grader who chooses soap making for a science fair project because a Procter & Gamble (P&G) company is nearby? The local library has everything it could find to develop an impressive collection on soap making and other personal care products, pet foods, and cleaning agents as a way to collaborate with the company. The library director invites P&G personnel to participate in reading contests, author events, and other activities as speakers, sponsors, judges, and participants. P&G presents programs twice a year at the library on topics such as, how to be a leader, how to succeed in business, and how to market your products. P&G donates funding to create an innovation lab at the library featuring 3-D printing, computer graphic art design and coding, video and music productions, and electrical circuitry.

Library staff and P&G representatives jointly present experiential learning and creative activities from Scratch and Arduino coding to squishy and paper circuitry to candle making. Their soap-making program includes the histories of techniques used from ancient times to Martha Stewart's "good, clean fun." The children's librarian mentors the eighth grader—guiding, nudging, and coaching her—to take advantage of the myriad resources and activities the library offers about soap making. In addition, this top-notch librarian connects the student with the P&G community liaison who opens up the company's archives of manuscripts, formulas, and actual products and their packaging. The history regarding the company and their products comes to life for the student. The experience of delving into the company's quality products and their marketing genius inspires the student to explore marketing and graphic art design as a career. The student wins first place in the fair.

The role of library staff could be to become highly skilled and capable of galvanizing young and old, rich and poor into higher levels of thinking, motivation, and accomplishment. We need to get excited, get collaborating, and most of all, get busy reinventing today's library. The joy of this endeavor is to look beyond the good that libraries have already done and seek out what we might do. To help society thrive, libraries may become tomorrow's community coach, if you will, to inspire the best and the brightest in each person.

## A Good Plan Embraces Progress

A bad plan fights progress. We may think we're planning for the future, but the future may surprise us with unexpected developments. Change for the sake of change is not helpful. Speculating, however, on what a library would look like a thousand years from now can stimulate our thinking and enable us to generate new ideas to make changes tied to the progress of humanity.

What will a library look like in an economically and spiritually depressed town? What will a library look like in a community with a high concentration of teachers or engineers or government workers or small business owners? How do we support a community and help it thrive no matter its starting point?

Two fathers in Dothan, Alabama, focused on helping the library renew itself. They envisioned that their city and county could become a place where their children would learn, grow, and stay as adults to serve. They created a good plan to start a grassroots effort that galvanized local businesses, government, and residents to secure funding to reinvent their library. Five years later, Dothan Houston County (AL) Library System won *Library Journal*'s LibraryAware Community Award (2015) for a renovated central library, two new branch libraries, reenergized staff, an exciting slate of programs, revitalized bookmobile service, and transformed community collaborations. Foot traffic at the central library jumped from 800 to 2,500 per day.[5]

Several libraries and schools across North America hold "Battle of the Books" reading contests for youth. It's important to note that no books are hurt before, during, or after a "battle"—the contest name is a reference to a satire written by Jonathan Swift and published as part of the introduction to his *A Tale of a Tub* in 1704. It depicts a literal battle between ideas and authors of books in the King's Library. Swift's concern was that the relatively new and more efficient technique of printing—the movable type method—would produce too many books promoting bad ideas.

Library staff track answers and add up scores at "Battle of the Books" reading contests. This "battle" (one of eight) is held in a high school gym; thirty-seven teams compete before six hundred cheering fans. Carroll County (MD) Public Library.

In the "battles" of today, students team up, read books, and answer questions in an energetic contest. "It is so great to see the level of excitement you normally see at a sporting event for an event about reading," says Irene Hildebrandt, media specialist supervisor, Carroll County (MD) Public Schools. Participation promotes greater depth and breadth of student reading; encourages cooperation and teamwork, as well as reading motivation and accomplishment. The larger goal is to promote richer comprehension and discussion of ideas. This is another example of good planning that produces the kind of results you want to see.

In Howard County, Maryland, thanks to A+ Partners in Education, 1,200 fifth-grade students participate in Battle of the Books—one-third of the county's fifth graders. The annual Friday-night extravaganza each April requires orchestrating five simultaneous "battles" for five thousand cheering fans. Teams (240 teams of five) read the same sixteen preassigned books, dream up a team name, such as, Book Bugs, Five Guys Books & Fries, Statues of Literacy, Chocolate Chip Bookies, then dress the part. "This A+ signature event inspires reluctant and avid readers alike because it's so much fun. Through reading a variety of genres and topics at all reading levels, students increase their reading comprehension and expand their horizons," notes Valerie Gross, CEO and president, Howard County (MD) Library System and Gale/*Library Journal* 2013 Library of the Year, adding, "The experience also teaches teamwork and leadership skills. Teams burst into cheer for each correct answer. Everybody wins!"

Jeff Ridgeway, children's librarian, Washington County (MD) Free Library, says, "The library, along with our schools and other partners, has created a community tradition—now in our 29th year—around the love of reading with Battle of the Books. It has become a rite of passage for generations of students in fourth, fifth, and sixth grades."

Angie Knight, Battle of the Books Committee Chair, Carroll County (MD) Public Library, adds, "Our collaboration has strengthened the bond between libraries and schools across the county. The library was looking for a way to better support our partner and great friend—the public school. This effort does that far beyond our original intention."

In Southport, Connecticut, the Pequot Library describes their mission as "Bringing Literature, Music, Art, Science & the Humanities to our Community." This good plan has four central components:

> **Children's Library:** With some of the best programs in the region, our children's library provides children with an ideal setting for fostering a lifelong love of learning.

Music for Youth, Pequot Library, Southport, CT. Enso Quartet master class with students Andrew Gray, Tomaso Scotti, and Zoie Chan.

**Nationally Important Special Collections:** Consisting of 30,000 items, our special collections are integrated into the day-to-day life of the library and in its exhibits and programs.

**Cultural Center:** Pequot is a true cultural center, with programs, concerts, exhibits, and lectures for the whole community. The Free Young Person's Concerts, which the library sponsors with Music for Youth, are just a few of the many cultural events at the highest level presented by Pequot.

**Circulating Collection:** At the heart of the library's day-to-day activities is its circulating collection of books and other materials in both print and electronic formats for all ages, which is managed for quality rather than size.[6]

In 1947, the Free Library of Philadelphia—we imagine to Benjamin Franklin's delight—started a collection of historic children's books. Their "Early American

Children's Books" and "Children's Literature Research Collection" are examples of good planning. Each collection uses a set of criteria for the development, maintenance, and use of the combined 78,000 rare and historic books. In addition, thirty-five Pennsylvania children's authors and illustrators have donated their original papers, manuscripts and illustrations, including Carolyn Haywood, illustrator and author of the "Eddie" and "Betsy" series that influenced generations of children in the mid-twentieth century.

Questions and points to ponder on distinguishing between a good and bad plan:

1. What might my library be doing that will lead to its extinction?
2. What might my library look like a thousand years from now? (Use this as a way to stimulate your thinking and the thinking of your colleagues—and to enable all of you to generate new ideas to make changes tied to the progress of humanity.)
3. Does my plan divorce itself from the past?
4. A successful library of the future is one that is in pursuit of identity. What is the real goal—and glory—of my library?
5. How can I improve a current plan or develop a new plan with regard to a collaborative effort?

### Notes

1. Samuel Woodworth, "The Meeting of the Waters of Hudson and Erie (lyrics)," 1825.
2. "Railroad History: An Overview of the Past," *American-Rails.com*, accessed April 2015, www.american-rails.com/railroad-history.html.
3. "Stalin's Five Year Plan," Spartacus Educational, accessed April 2015, http://spartacus-educational.com/RUSfive.htm.
4. "Ella Winter," Spartacus Educational, accessed April 2015, http://spartacus-educational.com/Aella_winter.htm.
5. John N. Berry III, "Transformed by the People: 2015 LibraryAware Community Award," *Library Journal* 140, no. 6 (April 1, 2015): 26–29.
6. Adapted from Music for Youth's website, accessed April 2015, www.musicforyouth.net/venues.html.

# 10

# PRACTICAL IMPLEMENTATION

*I can give you a six-word formula for success: Think things through—then follow through.*
**—EDDIE RICKENBACKER, WORLD WAR I FLYING ACE, FIRST CEO OF EASTERN AIR LINES**

████████ **"One of the mysterious things about growing is how we grow** from dependence to independence. Most everyone comes to an awareness of complete physical independence, but emotional independence is an altogether different matter. Some people seem to achieve so little emotional independence that their need for dependence gets in the way of their becoming all that they could be," said Fred Rogers, creator and host of Mister Rogers' Neighborhood.[1] How can we approach planning as maturely as possible to support our library and community? What is the essence of successful implementation? How would Mr. Rogers implement a plan?

Tanya Baronti Smith, program coordinator, Fred Rogers Center Early Learning Environment, says, "As we encourage young children to take time to settle the emotions in order to make thoughtful decisions, we as adults know that when we take time to reflect we are better able to plan and to carry out that plan."

Planning takes place in our minds but is grounded in our acts. How can we approach each situation with optimism and thoughtfulness? What assumptions need challenging? How does our concept of time play a role in carrying out a plan? What do we need to think through in order to successfully implement a project?

Although a formal "strategic" plan can be useful in terms of focusing us to set priorities, goals, and detailed objectives, the best plan—the plan behind the plan—may not seem to be a plan at all. A great plan seldom involves specifics. For example, Eddie Rickenbacker's plan—as president of Eastern Air Lines—was basically to get businesses and people flying. For twenty-five years, he successfully carried out that plan. Eastern was one of the top four airlines in the world, and for a time, the most profitable.

The purpose to enlighten humanity could be considered the overreaching philosophy for a library. This philosophy is implemented through everyday programs, activities, and services. The plan to fulfill this purpose could be described as "to encourage people to read in order to think, grow, and contribute to life." A good plan is timeless. No matter who sits in the director position, the plan can be implemented successfully. Getting people to think is a good plan today and will be a good plan fifty years from now and a thousand years from now. With rapid changes in technology, "reading" may look different in the future but reading in order to think, grow, and contribute to life is timeless.

One of today's catchphrases is about libraries helping people "to learn." Let's think about that for a moment. What if young adults are learning the wrong things, such as that it is acceptable to coast at work or to steal from a store because their friends are doing it? What if children are learning that they can get their way by being mean to a playmate? What if a person allows her shyness to overwhelm her and cannot effectively present in front of an audience, and therefore she "learns" and re-creates situations where she is unable to articulate ideas to a group? If we only learn to look for the negativity in each situation, how can we have eureka moments? How can we develop an "anything is possible" ethos? How can the twenty-first-century reinvention of libraries become a reality?

As Mrs. Banks, the popular character in the *Mary Poppins* novel, movie, and musical, might say:

> Come along, librarians, stand shoulder to shoulder with community partners in the fray. Think things through carefully as you implement your plan to get people to read and to think. We're in it for the long haul!
>
> Gather your resources. For a big project, you may need to work extra hard and find buttercups the size of saucers. For a small project, it may mean simply explaining your idea and getting only a few people to commit. Set

up a timetable, assign tasks, and empower everyone to get busy. Supply them with what they need and check in from time to time.

Dear me! Don't forget to add a spoonful of fun to get the job done.

## FOLLOW THROUGH

Timing and follow-through remind us of the importance of discovery #10. Part of learning right timing is discovering when it occurs. The comedian learns comedic right timing by focusing on the joke. Librarians learn right timing by focusing on the library's purpose and our goals and plans.

Can you imagine Shawn Achor's funny 2010 TED Talk on "The Happy Secret to Better Work" without right timing? Achor begins his talk with a childhood story of playing with his younger sister. He was seven years old; Amy was five. After Amy fell off his bunk bed and landed on "all fours," Achor tells his sister—as a way to prevent her from crying—"Hey, you landed on all fours, you must be a baby unicorn." It works. "Instead of crying . . . she smiled and scrambled onto the bed with all the grace of a baby unicorn . . ." (pause) ". . . with one broken leg."[2]

What about the award-winning performances of Victor Borge, Danish-American classical pianist and comedian: Borge was considered one of the masters of comic timing and follow-through. In Australia in 1962, he told his audience that he is flattered that their country's prime minister is in attendance in the concert hall. He says, "I have a habit of naming my dressing room after celebrities honoring me with their presence. And, since we were received so well by Sir Frank and Lady Tate—she has been so marvelous to my wife and myself—a very gracious hostess, I named my dressing room in honor of Lady Tate. I call it the Lady Room. Tonight we are honored by the presence of the prime minister and Dame Patty Menzies. And in honor of the prime minister, I'm going to change the name of the room from the Lady Room to the 'Mens-ie' Room."[3]

Focusing on the library director's plan to support the role of parents as first teachers, Carroll County (MD) Public Library staff refocused their efforts in the late 1990s and early 2000s. They evaluated what was working and what was not working. They sparked their own curiosity around finding ways to increase the ability of children's librarians to support families and create or expand optimal programs and family-friendly environments. They stepped up all efforts to build relationships with community partners and strengthen collaborations. The new mindset—to be poised and ready for right action—helped key staff recognize and take advantage of opportunities. In this way, the library discovered right timing for early childhood efforts. At each step of the way, such as retraining staff, redesigning storytimes, engaging parents, pursuing outside funds, designing a research study, welcoming families with new play-and-learn centers, and collaborating more effectively with local and state partners, library staff successfully harnessed their time. They rode the wave of right timing and increased their ability to follow through.

Time is not a part of life that we the authors think should be managed. It is a force to harness and becomes a partner in implementation. A plan such as getting people reading in order to think, grow, and contribute to life is a timeless plan, but harnessing our time to direct energy to making that happen is our challenge.

Suppose a disagreement surfaces between the fictional Herald City and Waldan County over the placement of a new library building when the recently elected and highly ambitious mayor, Joy Dogood, takes office. The library director, Rick Saunders, had previously won support from both county and city officials for the library to be located on six acres within city limits: a 48,000-square-foot building with plenty of parking and an outdoor park with performance stage—but not in the downtown area.

Mayor Dogood says to her staff, "I love libraries! I envision the new building as central to my downtown renaissance. I'm sure Rick will agree . . . or at least I don't think he'll fight me on this . . . or, er, I hope he won't." She calls her friend the governor to request participation in an urban economic development program. She and the governor belong to the same political party, one that is different than the county commissioners. Within a day, Mayor Dogood announces a $1.5 million grant to purchase three acres and to cover the cost of a new 25,000-square-foot library building in the heart of Herald City with only street parking. Her dream celebrates the library as a key part of an economic and cultural revival of the city. The problem is that her dream is really only a wish. Currently few residents live downtown, parking is always challenging, and an odd configuration of streets and old warehouse buildings will create a hidden entrance to the proposed library—one that requires walking through an alleyway.

That afternoon, Rick calls the offices of Waldan County commissioners and Mayor Dogood, inviting them to discuss their viewpoints that evening over a light dinner of pizza and salad. "Remember me," he says when Mayor Dogood answers, "I'm the library director!" Although the mayor blurts out that she has to answer another call, he continues to visualize in his mind that somehow—perhaps not right away—politics will be overruled by common sense.

Rick's staff members may not have fully studied his plan to get people reading in order to think and grow, but they understand the framework. His assistant director says, "Why don't you continue calling the mayor's office and gently nudge her to attend? I'll make sure everything is set up for the meeting and dinner." To everyone's surprise, the mayor shows up at the last minute.

Rick begins the meeting by saying, "Thank you for coming this evening. I am, above all, grateful and appreciative that the question is about—where to put the library—and not whether the community really wants or needs a library. Can we start our conversation by focusing on what each of you would like the library to do for you?"

*County commissioner #1:* "I'm the mother of three children. I'd like a library to offer a wide range of children's books, learning activities, and fun opportunities to create things in a 'no fail' space."

*Commissioner #2:* "I own an automotive repair shop and would like to partner with the library for community events like the jazz and apple harvest festivals and bring in an antique car show."

*Commissioner #3:* "I want a technology lab to explore all the latest gadgets, an auditorium for concerts, an outdoor stage for swing music and dance, and a monthly forum to discuss big ideas!"

*Mayor Dogood:* "I want those things too! It seems to me that the library will serve all families in the greater Herald City and Waldan County areas no matter if it's located in my preferred spot or yours. I know we will all take a risk to place it in today's downtown. It may take a long time before downtown becomes a flourishing destination, but the library can be a magnet to draw people in."

*Commissioner #1:* "But your track of land for the proposed library is half the size of what we have already secured a mile away. And it has no parking."

*Mayor Dogood:* "I have good news about the land and parking. Rick, I'm sorry I cut you short on the phone earlier. I got an unexpected call from an anonymous contributor that will enable us to purchase six acres—instead of three—and will allow for the construction of two downtown garages next to the library, giving the library a full parking garage with three hundred spaces, plus create an 800-square-foot library park and a 42,000-square-foot building."

The group unanimously votes to go with the mayor's idea. Over time, the city begins to grow and expand. It doesn't seem to work during the first few years, but slowly and steadily, if you pay close attention, you can see changes for the better. The library eventually becomes a local gem focused on supporting individuals, businesses, teens, and families with young children—all examples of plans within Rick's overarching plan. When the timing is right, the commissioners, Mayor Dogood, and Rick collaborate with the early childhood council to redesign the library to feature a large play-and-learn space for babies, toddlers, and preschoolers that offers a time for families to socialize and hang out together. A Library Express bookmobile is purchased to take programs, books, and computer tablets to schools, child-care settings, and homeschool families.

The follow-through work libraries do in collaboration with parents, agencies, and elected officials to support early learning and healthy social and emotional development is a plan within a plan. All staff members need a foundation of understanding about what their library offers families with young children and how they can support families. A children's librarian can have a higher level of expertise, but all staff should be poised and ready to interact with a family when the timing is right—during programs, in the stacks, or at the checkout desk.

Valerie Smirlock, communications manager for Delaware Stars, Delaware's Quality Rating and Improvement System at the University of Delaware, says, "Librarians have the perfect opportunity in storytime sessions, in the play and learn area, and at the checkout desk to shape interaction with children in such a way as to promote social and emotional skills. By connecting parents to local resources, librarians can also encourage parents as they help their young children develop self-regulation skills, the most important skills for children entering school." Smirlock, who is a former training coordinator on social and emotional early learning for the Maryland State Department of Education, adds, "Can the children sit still? Do they get along and share with others? Are they beginning to identify and express their emotions? Can they follow directions? Having these kinds of conversations with families in a non-threatening place like the library can effectively get more parents the kind of support they need around challenging behaviors and appropriate social and emotional skill building."[4]

## The Library Director Is Essential

Eddie Rickenbacker was the top American World War I fighter pilot. To jump-start his new airline company, Eastern Air Lines, in the 1930s, he bid zero cents per mile to win a US Postal Service contract for the Houston / Corpus Christi / Brownsville airmail route. Eastern grew into a top-performing, highly innovative company because Rickenbacker implemented his plan or primary intent—to get people flying. His successors, however, did not stay focused on that plan or purpose. Instead they became distracted by purchasing too many new planes, incurring debt, and grappling with organizational change. Within a generation, an unresolved union strike shut down the airline.[5]

Abraham Lincoln's original plan for reconstruction is another example of a great plan. He followed two guiding principles: "to accomplish the task [of reconstruction] as rapidly as possible and ignore calls for punishing the South."[6] As his biographer David Herbert Donald wrote,

> How the Southern states were to be governed during the transition from disunion to loyalty remained to be settled. Lincoln had now given up the idea of temporarily working with the rebel legislatures, admitting to the cabinet that he "had perhaps been too fast in his desires for early reconstruction."

But he felt strongly that the reorganization of these states could not be directed from Washington. "We can't undertake to run State governments in all these Southern States," he told his cabinet. "Their people must do that,—though I reckon that at first some of them may do it badly."

[Lincoln] "urged all the members to think carefully about the subject of reconstruction because 'no greater or more important one could come before us, or any future Cabinet.' 'There are men in Congress,' observed Lincoln, 'who, if their motives are good, are nevertheless impracticable, and who possess feelings of hate and vindictiveness' in which he did not sympathize and could not participate."[7]

After Lincoln's assassination, the people surrounding the president paid lip service to his plan, but they did not implement it.

When a director understands that the library is meant to encourage people to read so they can think and grow—perhaps without quite realizing it—all her energy goes toward following through to that end. Planning may not move from a concrete step A to step B to C then D, but the overarching plan should permeate every decision the director makes. As the library hires people, they are selected based on whether they can implement the plan. Children's librarians are hired to present storytimes and support parents in their role as first teacher—in order to prepare children to learn to read. Teen services librarians are hired to develop hands-on activities to get students excited about reading as a means to enrich life. Adult services staff are hired to work with individuals, businesses, and organizations to

Students use holographic diffraction grating glasses to take a unique look at everyday light and uncover some hidden imagery. Skokie (IL) Public Library.

get people reading to improve their skills and contribute more to life. Outreach librarians are hired to serve struggling families who don't use the library, to reach out to the homeless, the incarcerated, and the elderly—in order to get them reading to lift themselves up.

Feedback from library patrons, community partners, and colleagues determines how the plan will unfold. When a challenge arises—such as the Herald City and Waldan County scenario of competing interests for a new library location—a director automatically tuned into an overarching plan to fulfill the purpose of the library will help drive discussion to explore multiple solutions and find the best one for that time and place. As the project moves forward, listening to individuals, businesses, and groups will help the library do its best work for the community. Not paying attention to feedback can lead to failure. "For one, we stuck with the wrong strategy for too long," said Keith Nowak, describing the end of his start-up, Imercive. "I think this was partly because it was hard to admit the idea wasn't as good as I originally thought or that we couldn't make it work. If we had been honest with ourselves earlier on we may have been able to pivot sooner and have enough capital left to properly execute the new strategy. I believe the biggest mistake I made as CEO of Imercive was failing to pivot sooner."[8]

Fred Rogers's overarching plan might be described as: to help children—and adults—find ever-expanding playgrounds of the mind, body, and spirit.[9] All decisions he made for his educational television shows about which vocabulary words to emphasize, what song to sing, which puppet to use, and what message to convey stemmed from this idea—this plan—to help children grow up to be mature and productive and able to think for themselves.

Questions and points to ponder on plan implementation and follow-through:

1. Planning takes place in our minds but is grounded in our acts.
2. How can we approach each situation with optimism and thoughtfulness?
3. What assumptions need challenging?
4. How can we approach planning as maturely as possible to support our library and community?
5. How does our concept of time play a role in carrying out our plan?
6. What do we need to think through in order to successfully implement and follow through on a project?
7. Like Fred Rogers, how can we help children—and adults—find ever-expanding playgrounds of the mind, body, and spirit?

## Notes

1. Fred Rogers and Barry Head, *Mister Rogers' Playbook: Insights and Activities for Parents and Children* (Pittsburgh, PA: Family Communications, 1986), 73.

2. Shawn Achor, "The Happy Secret to Better Work," *TEDxBloomington*, filmed May 2011, www.ted.com/talks/shawn_achor_the_happy_secret_to_better_work.

3. "Victor Borge, Interviewed by Benny Lum (1962)," accessed May 2015, https://soundcloud.com/nfsaaustralia/victor-borge-interviewed-by.

4. Quoted in Dorothy Stoltz, "A Smorgasbord of Possibilities: How Maryland Libraries Address Their Charge," *Children and Libraries* 12, no. 2 (Summer 2014): 23.

5. "Eastern Airlines: History," accessed May 2015, http://easternairlines.aero/eastern-air-lines-history.html; and Stephen Sherman, "Capt. Eddie Rickenbacker: Top American Ace of WWI, 26 victories," AcePilots.com, August 2001, http://acepilots.com/wwi/us_rickenbacker.html.

6. "Lincoln Reconstruction Plan," *United States History*, accessed May 2015, www.u-s-history.com/pages/h177.html.

7. David Herbert Donald, *Lincoln* (London: Johnathan Cape Random House, 1995), 591–92.

8. Jamie Kingsbery, "33 Startups That Died Reveal Why They Failed," *Business Insider*, June 29, 2013, accessed May 2015, www.businessinsider.com/33-startups-that-died-reveal-why-they-failed-2013-6?op=1.

9. Rogers and Head, *Mister Rogers' Playbook*, 231.

# PART IV

# Engagement—The Heart of Collaboration

# 11

# GROWING AND FLOURISHING

*Without continual growth and progress, such words as improvement,*
*achievement, and success have no meaning.*

–BENJAMIN FRANKLIN

████████ **The Articles of Confederation–a demonstration of a poor plan–**
were replaced by the United States Constitution. Throughout the duration of the
Articles from 1781 to 1789, the thirteen states encountered many challenges, in
large part due to the governing oversight by the Congress of the Confederation.
The president of the Congress did not have the executive authority that came later
for the president of the United States under the Constitution.

Thomas Jefferson served as a delegate to the Congress of the Confederation
from Virginia and then as minister to France during this critical period. He writes
in his autobiography about several problems and how they were solved, such as
a committee's behavior of avoidance—not only avoiding discussion of issues but
members avoiding each other.

Jefferson describes how Benjamin Franklin tells a story during a debate to make a
point about getting along with each other in order to get things done. Dr. Franklin's

story: Two men lived in the Eddystone Lighthouse in the English Channel and shared duties. When supplies were delivered in the spring, the boatman discovered that the two keepers quarreled "soon after being left there [six months earlier at the remote lighthouse], had divided into two parties, assigned the cares below to one, and those above to the other, and had never spoken to, or seen, one another since."[1]

As Robert Burns said in his 1785 poem, "To a Mouse" after ploughing a field and accidentally destroying a mouse nest:

> The best laid schemes o' Mice an' Men
> Gang aft agley,
> An' lea'e us nought but grief an' pain,
> For promis'd joy![2]

Just having a good plan doesn't guarantee good results. People who rely on plans alone—whether it is a strategic plan, project plan, action plan, master plan, executive plan, performance plan, or one for marketing, business, staff development, risk management, building, technology, or a contingency plan, a floor plan, a lesson plan, a game plan, a retirement plan, a health plan, a life plan, a funeral plan, a low-carb diet plan, or a community plan—may end up like the mouse without a house or the keepers of the Eddystone lighthouse.

Avoiding problems—and each other—does little to help a collaboration succeed. Community outreach and collaborative efforts require the time for staff members to be able to listen and respond to individuals, families, and businesses. Dr. Judi Moreillon, Texas Woman's University, School of Library and Information Studies, and author of *Coteaching Reading Comprehension Strategies in Elementary School Libraries: Maximizing Your Impact*, says, "People working in the libraries of today and tomorrow need administrative permission to establish professional relationships with representatives of other organizations and businesses. They need to go into the community as a 'listener.' In order to see how they can connect the library to support their community, librarians need to say, 'This is how we can work with you to help you reach your goals.' In this way, the library becomes a leader in specific ways within each community—economically, civically, educationally, or culturally."

DISCOVERY #11

## MEET CHALLENGES

A successful library meets challenges and overcomes or works through or goes around obstacles in order to help the organization and the community grow and flourish. A library may think about growth in terms of adding staff members, branches, and partnerships or increasing floor space and collection size or boosting program and service statistics, but growth means flourishing in the right way for your community. Don't let traditions limit your thinking in these ways. Meeting challenges ignites growth. The growth of a library means making the right things happen in order to support the enlightenment of humanity in your neighborhood—through overcoming everyday obstacles and offering top-notch activities tailored for *your* customers, such as storytimes for children, makerspaces for teens, and book discussion programs for adults. How can the library fulfill its community role and meet challenges in meaningful ways?

Librarians can invest financial resources wisely by asking smart planning questions regularly—what's working and what can be done differently to be more effective. An astute investment is more than spending money judiciously; it means librarians devoting time, skills, creativity, and integrity.

Sari Feldman, Cuyahoga County (OH) Public Library executive director and ALA president 2015–16, says, "As libraries focus on finding and training qualified staff that inspire and support self-directed learning, they connect with individuals,

Little Movers storytime. La Crosse (WI) Public Library.

businesses, and organizations. When library staff think of users asking, 'What can the library do for me?' they build trust in their communities. Public libraries are natural connectors for families. We need to support those trusting families by providing opportunities for community building within our branches. Programs that build parent engagement should not only address school issues but should also encourage the development of camaraderie within the group. Storytimes should not only teach early literacy skills but also offer time for parents to socialize. Entrepreneur classes should include opportunities for participants to pitch their ideas and even test their product. Public libraries need to take a more active role in developing themselves as gathering places for open discussion, innovation, and learning to help their communities flourish."

Services and activities can be revamped, refocused, and remarketed as appropriate. Feedback from partnerships and collaborations can help libraries add new life to their purpose. Nina Lindsay, Oakland (CA) Public Library children's services coordinator and ALSC Education Committee Chair 2014–15, says, "By investing time up front to build relationships with partnering agencies and coalitions—although it may not be an obvious or immediate path for successful results—a long-term trust between library and partnering agency can build and eventually thrive. What are our partner's needs, challenges, limitations, and strengths? Can we take the time to visit their sites, talk and listen to them? Find out what support they would appreciate the most. How can we help them meet *their* challenges?"

In reaching out to families who do not use the library—especially families struggling economically—Maryland libraries are experimenting with a library café program. This discussion program is adapted from ideas used in the World Café method of group dialogue, but the library program focuses discussion on the excitement of learning—as opposed to more social work–type topics, such as how to discipline your child. Library cafés invite parents for a deeper discussion about learning for themselves as adults and learning for their children. For example, parents can discuss the progression of how children develop writing skills. Babies enjoy squeezing playdough, which strengthens their fingers and hands as a first step toward the process of writing. Then it's step by step—children begin to scribble, make letter- and number-like shapes, then advance to making letters and numbers. Parents have aha moments in the informal and fun café atmosphere and are excited to share their observations and ideas. The discussion closure question invites feedback, "what can the library do for you and your family?"[3]

Talking to Kris Peters, who is a retired librarian with Carroll County (MD) Public Library and a weaver, it is easy to see how weaving can be a powerful metaphor for library service. Like weaving, libraries strive to develop a well-functioning process while creating a work of art. Weavers listen to the fabric to determine when to press gently and when to pull. We as librarians can listen to our customers to know when to press gently to encourage learning and when to pull to promote taking risks. No matter what kind of fiber a weaver uses—alpaca fleece, linen, or lamb's wool—a rhythm is established specific to the fabric woven. Librarians can cultivate different rhythms for serving people of all fibers and fabrics—and watch each masterpiece unfold.

We need not look for an example of an inspired collaboration other than the growth of the American colonies into a group of states under the Articles of Confederation then into a united group of states under the Constitution. They learned how to take risks, how to grapple with differing viewpoints, how to maintain momentum, and how to learn from mistakes and meet challenges in order to grow and flourish. As Jefferson says in his autobiography, "During the war of Independence . . . the spirit of the people . . . urged them to zealous exertions . . . but when peace and safety were restored, and every man became engaged in useful and profitable occupation, less attention was paid to [whether the Articles were working or not working]."[4]

In the end, a plan that resulted in an ineffective collaboration was peaceably discarded to design a better plan, the Constitution—one that is thought through and produces positive results.

Questions and points to ponder on meeting challenges, and growing and flourishing as an organization and as a community collaboration:

1. The growth of a library means making the right things happen in order to support the enlightenment of humanity—in practical ways—in my neighborhood. What does this mean to me? Early literacy programs? Book discussion groups? Makerspaces? How can I help my library fulfill this community role and grow and develop as an organization in meaningful ways?
2. How can I work with other organizations or businesses to be a part of their goal for the community while at the same time fulfilling the library's purpose?
3. By asking people in and outside the library setting, "What can the library do for you?" or "What more can the library do for you and your family?" I up the ante that my organization will grow and flourish.
4. What are my partners' needs, challenges, limitations, and strengths? Can I take the time to visit my partner locations, talk and listen to their administration and staff? How can I help them meet *their* challenges? (Find out what support they would appreciate the most.)
5. To borrow from Benjamin Franklin's story about getting along with each other: How goes it, friend? How is your companion? Have not you seen him or her today? Have you forgotten or ignored someone?

## Notes

1. Adrienne Koch and William Peden, eds., *The Life and Selected Writings of Thomas Jefferson* (New York: The Modern Library, 2004), 54–55.
2. From Robert Burns, "To a Mouse," www.poetryfoundation.org/poem/173072.
3. Adapted from Dorothy Stoltz, Paula Isett, Linda Zang, Liza Frye, and Liz Sundermann, "Just Good Practice," *Public Libraries* 54 no. 5 (September/October 2015): 27–30.
4. Adrienne Koch and William Peden, ed., *The Life and Selected Writings of Thomas Jefferson* (New York: Modern Library, 2004), 75.

# 12

# SPARKING CURIOSITY

*The mind is not a vessel to be filled, but a fire to be kindled.*

–PLUTARCH

**■■■■■■■ Does your library create opportunities to spark aha moments?**
A library is designed to spark curiosity in individuals and in the community. Do you provoke library patrons of all ages to shout *Eureka* every time they have a great idea? Do your customers say that you are serving their needs? Is there a recognition by patrons that they are nailing down their "aha moments" because of how you spark their curiosity?

A research study conducted in an elementary school library explored the topic of fostering curiosity. Sherry R. Crow, Ph.D., associate dean of school library science and educational media at the University of Nebraska at Kearney, examined how adults—parents, teachers, and school librarians—influence students' intrinsic motivation for information seeking. In her 2007 study, Dr. Crow asked the question: What has happened in the lives of students who exhibit a boundless zest for learning?

[Children's] little wiggling bodies showed their excitement every time they visited the library. Simple questions about almost any topic, from bugs to trains . . . elicited lively responses that stimulated them to look for facts on the Web and in books . . . Some students continue to be curious [throughout elementary school]. Their pursuit seems endless and insatiable, regardless of the external demands of the educational system. What has happened in the lives of these students to keep the curiosity fires burning [while other students' zest for learning diminishes]?[1]

Crow discovered that "all of the children in the study experienced what I've termed a point-of-passion experience: an event that triggered months—and sometimes years—of interest and in-depth information seeking about a topic. For many of the children [often starting at age four and five years old], adult attention turned these

Awarding-winning bookmobile program ignites curiosity for students. SPARK (Students Progress and Achieve with Reading Kits) program partners with area Title One fifth graders for a bookmobile visit. Professional librarians assist students to select five books to keep, read, and swap with friends for the entire summer, fine free, in advance of starting middle school. Cecil County (MD) Public Library.

events into information seeking passions . . . Some of the effort was just paying attention long enough to help the child [do an activity] . . . Though it may seem that peers have more sway, the active adult relationships in students' lives appear to be more influential."[2]

How can libraries support the development of curiosity in children and adults as well as businesses and organizations? Elliott Masie, learning technology expert, producer, and author, told a group of Maryland librarians to get into the business of curiosity management. In that way, people coming into libraries will be supported in their curiosity and can get turned onto learning. Masie asked, "How can you delight your customers? People can get turned on to learning at a library. Do not emulate the school—although schools can do great stuff, the public library has a different DNA, a different vibration. Create positive experiences at the library so people will want to come back and will recommend their friends to come to the library. Will it be a great decision for them to have come to the library?"[3]

In his essay "On Listening to Lectures," Plutarch, first-century Greek philosopher and historian, wrote, "But as for those lazy persons . . . let us urge them that, when their intelligence has comprehended the main points, they put the rest together by their own efforts, and use their memory as a guide in thinking for themselves, and, like taking a seed, develop and expand it. For a mind does not require filling like a bottle, but rather, like wood, it only requires kindling to create in it an impulse to think independently and an ardent desire for the truth."[4]

The most effective plan is one that the library director (and staff) strive to implement each day: How can the library kindle a symbolic bonfire of the mind?" The director and senior staff members model how to activate the organization's best skills and talents to fulfill the plan to enlighten humanity in practical, everyday ways—to stimulate curiosity. How can the fire of lifelong learning be kindled in each community? How can curiosity be ignited in each person? If a library cannot spark curiosity or challenge the community to think—with all of its excellent books, programs, and staff—then what or who will?

Too often, library staff development trainings or educational classes seek to transmit knowledge or fill one's mind with facts and "crucial information." While knowledge, facts, and instruction are important and should not be overlooked, the heart of effective staff development and education for today's library workers is helping them *learn to think*. Learning to think effectively is multifaceted—learning how to learn, unlearn, and relearn, and how to challenge deeper thought and reflection in those practical, everyday ways.

How can library staff members be trained or educated to develop their best skills and talents in order to stimulate curiosity in themselves as well as in individuals and groups in their community? How can they apply those skills to help community partnerships succeed—and thus impact the library's effectiveness in the community?

The joy of sharing books. Pierce County (WA) Public Library. *Photo by Chris Tumbusch.*

One effective way is to keep things light and use a bit of humor. Besides physical health benefits—such as lowering blood pressure and increasing vascular blood flow—laughing improves learning, creativity, and memory. The ability to laugh leads to the ability to stay above the fray. This skill leads to the ability to maintain a sense of curiosity and to think at deeper levels. Laughing can help us minimize taking life too seriously and boost our ability to think.

Thomas Jefferson described Benjamin Franklin using good humor as he made a point after a long debate. The smaller States initially opposed the passing of the Articles of Confederation in 1781, believing that they would be swallowed up by the large states.

Dr. Franklin . . . observed that "at the time of the union of England and Scotland, the Duke of Argyle was most violently opposed to that measure, and among other things predicted that, as the whale had swallowed Jonah, so Scotland would be swallowed by England. However," said the Doctor, "when Lord Bute came into the government, he soon brought into its administration so many of his countrymen, that it was found in event that Jonah swallowed the whale." This little story produced a *general* laugh, and restored good humor, and the article of difficulty was passed.[5]

# LEARN TO THINK-EFFECTIVELY

Let's explore four innovative ideas on creativity and organizational learning to help libraries embrace curiosity or what Thomas Hobbes described as "the lust of the mind." See appendix H for suggested reading.

## Asking the Right Questions

Peter Senge, American systems scientist and author of *The Fifth Discipline: The Art and Practice of the Learning Organization*, developed five learning disciplines: shared vision, mental models, personal mastery, team learning, and systems thinking. He founded the Society for Organizational Learning, North America. Like the corporations and businesses that Senge inspired, libraries can embrace change as a catalyst for continuous learning and improvement. Making the right things happen means asking the right questions on a regular basis and pondering the answers. For example:

What's working well?

What is not working?

What can we do differently to be more effective?

## De Bono's Six Thinking Hats

Edward de Bono, a Maltese physician, originator of the term *lateral thinking*, and author of *Six Thinking Hats*, developed an outstanding approach to effective thinking. He writes,

A major corporation (ABB) used to spend twenty days on their multinational project team discussions. Using the parallel thinking of the Six Hats method, the discussions can now take as little as two days. A researcher from a top IBM laboratory told me that the Six Hats method had reduced meeting times to one quarter of what they had been. Statoil in Norway had a problem with an oil rig that was costing about one hundred thousand dollars a day. A certified trainer, Jens Arup, introduced the Six Hats method and in twelve minutes the problem was solved—and the one-hundred-thousand-a-day expenditure was reduced to nil . . . In a simple experiment with three hundred senior public servants, the introduction of the Six Hats method increased thinking productivity by 493 percent.[6]

What is the essence of De Bono's method? A quick outline demonstrates how to evoke different parts of our thinking abilities:

1. White hat = gathering facts and objective information (scientist's white coat)
2. Red hat = eliciting feelings, mood, and intuition ("heart" of feelings)
3. Black hat = questioning why an idea may not work; inspiring a devil's-advocate approach (black-robed judge)
4. Yellow hat = looking for possible opportunities, benefits, and rewards (positive "sunny" outlook)
5. Green = finding new, creative ideas (new shoots of grass)
6. Blue = "master" hat to control the thinking process, getting an overview and creating a summary (overarching sky)

This approach can be done individually or in groups. Think of an issue or a problem you want to solve, or think of an idea or a plan you'd like to implement. Express it in one sentence.

1. Choose a hat to begin. Often, this is the blue one, for how you should think about it. For example, what feelings (fears) need to be considered? What about future consequences? What do we need to learn first?

2. Go through all six hats and keep notes on your observations
   a. White: What facts do I need and how do I get them?
   b. Red: How do I feel about all of this?
   c. Black: What are the risks? Worst-case scenario?
   d. Yellow: What are all the possible advantages/benefits? What is the best possible outcome?

## SAMPLE SIX-HAT ISSUES

1. Although one of the library's priorities is serving children birth to age five and their parents and caregivers, the mayor's new million-dollar early learning initiative does not include the library.

2. How can we cover the information desk schedule while at the same time giving staff members the flexibility to attend early childhood coalition meetings?

3. Computer tablets, smart phones, and verbal command devices are increasingly becoming a part of daily life; how can librarians become media mentors to families supporting them as they develop their own best practices?

4. The library—a neutral entity—is a terrific place for small and large group meet-ups for people to discuss topics of interest, formally and informally, but few groups are using my library in that way.

5. How can we spark curiosity and support people of all ages as they pursue their interests?

6. How do we involve a major sponsor—who wants to participate in design of a new play-and-learn area—in a pragmatic way without losing control of our vision?

    e.   Green: What new approaches can I generate? How can I see this problem in a new way?

    f.   Blue: Review and sum up what I have learned in this process. Next step?

For more information, see "Suggested Reading," appendix H, for a list of Dr. Edward de Bono's books.

## Reading Great Literature

One of the best ways to stimulate the mind and spark curiosity is to read great literature, poetry, mythology, and philosophy, such as Parmenides and Elizabeth Barrett Browning. Jamie Littlefield, instructional designer, teacher, and writer, says,

> The great books were written by some of the best minds in history. By reading them, your own mind can expand and your thoughts reach a higher plane. Sir Richard Livingston [vice chancellor, Oxford University, 1944–47] said:

"We are tied down, all our days and for the greater part of our days, to the commonplace. This is where contact with great thinkers, great literature helps. In their company we are still in the ordinary world, but it is the ordinary world transfigured and seen through the eyes of wisdom and genius."

Reading the great books may not turn us into Platos and Einsteins. But, their words can bring out our strengths.[7]

How does your library promote great literature and great thinkers? Do you offer a place for people to meet up to discuss, ponder, and appreciate works such as *Treasure Island*, *The Adventures of Huckleberry Finn*, or *The Iliad and the Odyssey*? Can you hold roundtable conversations on a Shakespeare play or the poetry of Edgar Allan Poe and Emily Dickinson featuring skits and recitations performed by local middle and high school students? Are small independent groups clamoring to schedule library space to talk about how to turn theoretical philosophy into everyday practical terms, using Emerson's *Essay on Self-Reliance* or Plato's *The Allegory of the Cave* or Pope's *Essay on Criticism*? Do you see the faces of children lighting up with a sense of discovery in your library's storytimes and reading nooks?

## Leading from Any Position

How can libraries adapt Peter Senge's principles? Becky Schreiber and John Shannon offer trainings to help libraries be their best.[8] One such training, called "Leading from Any Position," is designed to help library workers from all levels jump-start their ability to apply the learning organization principles, which include shared vision, mental models, personal mastery, team learning, and systems thinking.

Catherine DiCristofaro, Charlotte Hall branch manager, St. Mary's County (MD) Library, says,

> When I took *Leading from Any Position*, I wanted to create a collection of take-home story and activity packets as a ready-made resource for English language learners to use with their children to promote early literacy skills. The training helped me to reflect on the director's priorities, identify a customer need, pinpoint ways to fulfill it, and make a pitch for my project idea.
>
> I learned to review the library's strategic plan and ask questions such as, what opportunities already exist for the library to do more for an individual or group? I focused on the goal to "continue to use and reach new target groups with our Every Child Ready to Read workshops and information." We were able to build on a partnership with the literacy council that already existed and help potential customers find useful library resources.[9]

Another training participant, Jennifer Spriggs, Allegheny County Library System, says, "By creating ground rules for a work team, I learned we can perform more efficiently and effectively. Asking useful questions can move the group towards a decision: Are we ready to make a decision? What do we need to make a decision? What decision have we made? What actions are required? Who is going to do them and by when? One of my favorite 'aha moments' was hearing the statement—Where you focus your attention, your energy will follow."[10]

How can libraries create and nurture new leaders—at all levels—to redesign today's libraries and to develop effective community collaborations? Paula M. Singer, PhD, CEO/chief strategist, the Singer Group, says, "Give [employees] opportunities to show leadership even if they are not in a management role yet. Allow them to cross train others . . . or create mentor partner programs where they are paired up with others in the organization and they can coach each other. In the end, the responsibility for the growth of our employees is ours. We have to provide the environment, tools, and coaching required to grow our next leaders."[11]

Studying great leaders is another way to learn how to spark curiosity and think effectively. A couple examples of leaders who were constantly improving themselves and their ability to think and contribute to life include George Washington and Benjamin Franklin.

Jefferson wrote,

> When Dr. Franklin went to France, on his revolutionary mission, his eminence as a philosopher, his venerable appearance, and the cause on which he was sent, rendered him extremely popular. For all ranks and conditions of men there, entered warmly into the American interest. He was, therefore, feasted and invited into all the court parties. At these he sometimes met the old Duchess of Bourbon, who, being a chess player of about his force, they very generally played together. Happening once to put her king into prize, the Doctor took it. "Ah," said she, "we do not take kings so." "We do in America," said the Doctor.[12]

Questions and points to ponder on sparking curiosity, becoming a thriving organization, and learning how to think:

1. What's working well?
2. What is not working?
3. What can we do differently to be more effective?
4. Asking useful questions can move the group toward a decision: Are we ready to make a decision? What do we need to make a decision? What decision have we made? What actions are required? Who is going to do them and by when?

5. Is this statement an aha moment for you: Where I focus my attention, energy will follow.

6. How can libraries be the go-to place for tools to spark curiosity, support creativity, and develop the mind?

## Notes

1. Sherry Crow, *Exploring the Experience of Upper Elementary School Children Who Are Intrinsically Motivated to Seek Information*, PhD diss., Emporium University, Kansas, December 2008, published in 2009.

2. Sherry R. Crow, "Fostering the Curiosity Spark," *School Library Monthly* 26, no. 5 (January 2010): 50–52.

3. Teleconference interview with Elliott Masie, Transformation Group meeting, convened by the Division of Library Development and Services, Maryland State Department of Education, May 26, 2015.

4. Babbit Plutarch, *Moralia*, vol. 1, trans. Frank Cole (Cambridge, MA: Harvard University Press, 1927), 257–59.

5. Adrienne Koch and William Peden, eds., *The Life and Selected Writings of Thomas Jefferson* (New York: Modern Library, 2004), 166–67.

6. Edward De Bono, preface to *Six Thinking Hats,* revised and updated (New York: Back Bay Books, 1999).

7. Jamie Littlefield, "10 Ways Reading the Great Books Can Improve Your Life: The Master Course in Personal Development May Already Be Sitting On Your Shelf," *Self Made Scholar.org*, March 4, 2009, http://selfmadescholar.com/b/2009/03/04/10 -ways-reading-the-great-books-can-improve-your-life/.

8. See their website, http://schreibershannon.com.

9. Catherine DiCristofaro, "Past Participant Action Plans—New LFAP," *Leading from Any Position* (wiki), action plans from December 2012 workshop, http://lfap.pbworks .com/w/page/62130310/Past%20Participant%20Action%20Plans%20-%20New %20LFAP; and e-mail interviews by the author.

10. Jennifer Spriggs, "Leading from Any Position 1," *Western Maryland Regional Library Learning Journal Blog*, April 13, 2009.

11. "Stuck in Place," Singer Group, September 19, 2012, www.singergrp.com/blog/2012/ 09/19/stuck-in-place/.

12. Koch and Peden, *Writings of Thomas Jefferson*, 167.

# 13

# ENGAGING YOUR COMMUNITY

*I don't believe in mass communication . . . The space between two people is holy ground.*
−FRED ROGERS

██████████ **Good libraries are not always those with large square footage** or big budgets. You don't have to be located in an affluent neighborhood. You can be anywhere in the world. Great libraries are created by the people who work in them, by implementing the purpose or plan for a library—to help enlighten humanity by challenging people to think for themselves and develop their best skills.

One example of what great library service looks like is in rural Montana. Molly Ledermann, one of the 2013 winners of the I Love My Librarian! award, says, "Libraries help people to help themselves, and that makes their lives better."[1] Molly is a reference librarian at the Missoula (MT) Public Library. Caroline Reed, a library patron, states, "To every facet of her work, Molly brings tremendous creativity and a spirit of collaboration and fun. Throughout, she inspires everyone around her to do his or her best . . . As I have gotten to know Molly better, I have also learned about her efforts to make the library a friendlier place, from the patron's perspective. For instance, when the library underwent a redesign of the reference area, Molly was adamant that the library create a space for patrons to interact with the librarian, face-to-face. Now, the reference desk is a place where I can sit down and have a great conversation."[2]

Katie Stanton, Missoula Art Museum marketing director, describes Molly's approach to service: "Molly's unlimited curiosity has led to community programming that links . . . art to the art of the written word. She has produced programs that unite the Missoula Art Museum (MAM) and the Missoula Public Library as community partners for the benefit of the people in our community . . . She challenged us to think large and collaboratively [producing joint exhibits and programs beyond what we thought possible]."[3]

How do you engage people in your community who come to the library and those who do not?

# ONE PERSON AT A TIME

Whether it is face-to-face or online communication, engaging the community one person at a time is the most effective way to stimulate curiosity and support lifelong learning. No matter the age, income, or education level of the person, libraries can strive to serve the people in the community in neutral, safe-to-fail environments. One person at a time means that the pace of sparking curiosity and promoting creative thinking may be slow, but it can be steady. Let's take a peek.

## Hire Staff with Compassion

The room is humming with excitement and delight. Parents and children, library staff, and community partners are chattering away and enjoying dinner together. Afterward, the kids skip into the next room for play activities. A mother proudly tells her library story: "Being homeless a few short years ago, I got into the routine of bringing my children into the library each day. One day, before we got to the library, Miss Sue [from the checkout desk] was walking down the street on her lunch break. She greeted us: 'Hello, how are you? Will we see you in the library later today?' She talked to us as if we were any other family that goes to the library. That conversation was a turning point in my life. I began to think of myself in a more optimistic and confident way. In time, I was able to get out of a troubled marriage and move into an apartment with my children."[4]

This true story shows how far a gesture of goodwill and compassion can lead and the power and potential of libraries to touch local communities. This "library café" program is a discussion program loosely based on Illinois's Strengthening Families model, Love Is Not Enough Parent Cafés. These programs exemplify the effort by libraries to engage families in new and refreshing ways. Library conversation starters are designed to help parents focus discussion around lifelong learning and how to convey their excitement of learning to their children. It's also a golden opportunity to ask parents how can the library better serve families.[5]

## Express Cheerfulness and Kindness

"Think about what a public library means to kids on the fringe," says Regina Calcaterra, *New York Times* best-selling author of *Etched in Sand: A True Story of Five Siblings Who Survived an Unspeakable Childhood on Long Island.* She smiles as she recalls the enjoyment of reading and visiting the library as a child. "There were times my brother, sisters, and I would go to the library all day. I grew up with a mentally ill mother in the 1960s and '70s. She left me and my siblings alone for long periods of time, often homeless or in houses without electricity or running water. We learned to take care of ourselves. On the one hand the library gave us a safe, positive environment with the basics—heat/AC, running water, a bathroom. On the other hand, we could read quietly and be inspired to create a better life."[6]

Regina is now an attorney for the state of New York and writes in her book,

> At a library table we play Mad Libs and muse through the *Highlights* magazines together. When the kids [my young brother and sister] are quietly wrapped in their storybooks, I find myself living with my favorite characters in the worlds of Judy Blume novels. I don't care that I've already read [them all.] . . . I also go through every biography they have on Amelia Earhart, my heroine. Amelia was brave and courageous. She didn't let others limit her dreams and she never took no for an answer. Amelia Earhart made her own

Regina Calcaterra speaks about her best-selling memoir, *Etched in Sand*, at Middle Country Public Library, Long Island, NY.

rules . . . Books are the only escape I have from our struggles. I know one day Rosie [my baby sister] will need that escape, too, so I always sign out library books to read to her. My favorites to share are from the Landmark Books series, about our country's founders. Before bed, Rosie snuggles in as I read to her about Betsy Ross, Dolley Madison, and Pocahontas.[7]

Regina adds in an interview, "Librarians may not think they can establish influential relationships with disconnected youth because they don't spend hours with children and teens the way teachers do. I believe that no child is a lost cause. It doesn't matter if you know the child's struggles, be there for that moment in time. Each moment of kindness—from many caring adults—added up and helped me create self-worth and determination. For example, I remember a school crossing guard taught me how to blow my nose and a friend's mother gave me a new toothbrush. My childhood interactions with kind and cheerful library staff helped me build self-esteem—I was treated with respect. In their quiet ways, they helped me develop a love of reading and learning, opening me to a world of possibility."

## Offer a Smorgasbord of Learning Tools

Colin Rice, a homeschooled student, spends many hours at the Craig Public Library on Prince of Wales Island in Alaska. A cheerful eleven-year-old, he enjoys the library's fun technology programs and other resources; for example, "attending video conferences, reading books, and participating in gaming and [computer] coding events," according to the Institute of Museum and Library Services. Colin is becoming a local expert on 3-D printing, helping to assemble the new printer, demonstrating how to use it, and exploring its benefits to humanity. Colin says, "I know this library has helped instill in my mind and heart what can be done to broaden not just my own horizons, but those of others. When I travel I will first look for the local library, always."[8] Craig (AK) Public Library was a 2015 winner of the National Medal for Museum and Library Service.

## Saying Yes!

Let's take a look at an admittedly fictional "Inspiration Point Library": a library in some small town with, say, less than 850 people. Anita, the circulation clerk, and Bryan, the librarian, work side-by-side at the service desk. Anita and Bryan have different skill sets and work as a team to provide the best service possible. They established a customer service approach based on the inquiry: What can the library do for you?

On some days, they become a little impatient with their limited resources or with what seems like people taking advantage of their good nature. They enjoy, however, sparking curiosity in themselves and others. It's been important to them to think about how the library can better serve each individual. Out of their ponderings and conversations, they create an organizational culture with the goal to strive to say yes—where reasonable—to individuals and organizations who ask for information or bring an idea to the library. They tease each other about their friendly competition to avoid writing in the library's "no log"—that is, an ongoing list describing what and why they said no to a library patron. They use the no log to reflect on how to constantly improve service with little or no extra funding.

One day Joanne, new to the neighborhood, strolls into the library and describes herself as an author of books that might interest people in the community: cookbooks, hiking, and chicken-soup-for-the-soul-type children's stories. Some inner–Debby Downer voice is having a hissy fit inside Anita and Bryan: "Alert, alert! This person may end up taking a lot of your time without producing good statistical results." They squelch the Debby Downer voice and cheerfully and sincerely welcome Joanne to the library, asking her to drop off some of her books. Joanne leaves her business card.

The next day, Bryan searches to find whether Joanne is featured on the Internet. He discovers that Joanne works for a florist in the city and has penned a dozen books. He tells Anita, "Joanne's books are printed by a small publisher or are self-published, but they sound pretty neat. They're listed on Amazon and Goodreads with mostly four- and five-star ratings. I'd like to take a chance and ask Joanne to be part of our 'Farm to Fork' program. She could give a talk on this one: *I Didn't Have Paprika, So I Substituted Another Spice Cookbook: How to Cook with Whatever Is in the Pantry.* Gosh, look at this book title for kids: *I Want to Dance Like an Astronaut.* She sounds like a lot of fun!"

Joanne becomes a regular library user and often asks Bryan and Anita to give feedback on her book projects. They enjoy provoking Joanne to "spice up" her writing. You can hear Bryan saying, "Joanne, this chapter is too bland. Do you want your readers to stop reading?" Anita chimes in, "Pages 35–37 are BOR-ing!" Joanne attends a classic-book discussion led by Bryan each month. Anita and Joanne co-facilitate the library café for parents and children. Their goal is to spark the imagination of adults and children. They use books to get participants to think about ideas, provide new fun technology to try out, and offer other exciting things to do and ways to make each other laugh.

Ten years later, Joanne's first teen novel, *I Want to Be a Dragon, Don't You?*, becomes an international best seller. She launches her book tour—with Bryan and Anita by her side—at the Inspiration Point Library. Bryan and Anita are interviewed by the *Today* show, the *New York Times*, and Waldo, a new online social network service. In Joanne's widely viewed TED Talk about creative writing, she describes Inspiration

Point Library as "the community hub for motivating people and sparking curiosity about the wonders of life." Donations come pouring into the little library. Anita and Bryan first dance like astronauts, then get busy expanding their programs and services beyond what they ever thought possible.

Points to ponder about engaging the people in your community:

1. One person at a time means that the pace of sparking curiosity and promoting creative thinking may be slow, but it can be steady.
2. No matter my library's size or budget, am I hiring staff who can spark curiosity in themselves and others, who are compassionate and cheerful, and who have a can-do attitude?
3. No matter my library's size or budget, what am I doing to feature new and exciting learning tools?
4. Does my library have a "no log" and strive to say yes to every patron inquiry or idea?
5. What is my library doing to be the community hub for motivating people and sparking curiosity about the wonders of life?

## Notes

1. The Carnegie Corporation of New York/*New York Times* I Love My Librarian! award encourages library users to recognize the accomplishments of exceptional public, school, college, community college, or university librarians. For more information, go to www.ilovelibraries.org/lovemylibrarian.
2. Caroline Reed, library patron, "Nominations for: Molly E. K. Ledermann," "I Love My Librarian! 2013 Award," 1, www.ilovelibraries.org/sites/default/files/nominations -molly-ledermann.pdf.
3. Katie Stanton, Marketing and Communications Director, Missoula Art Museum, ibid., 2–3.
4. This story is adapted from Dorothy Stoltz, "A Smorgasbord of Possibilities: How Maryland Libraries Address Their Charge," *Children and Libraries* 12, no. 2 (Summer 2014): 21.
5. Ibid.
6. Regina Calcaterra speaking to the Carroll County (MD) Early Childhood Consortium and other agencies, March 27, 2015.
7. Regina Calcaterra, *Etched in Sand: A True Story of Five Siblings Who Survived an Unspeakable Childhood on Long Island* (New York: William Morrow, 2013), 38–42.
8. "Craig Public Library, Craig, AK" (press release), Institute of Museum and Library Services, June 2015, www.imls.gov/news/2015_medals_craig_public_library.aspx.

# 14

# IT'S MAGIC!

*Everyone can perform magic, everyone can reach his goals, if he is able to think.*

**–HERMANN HESSE**

**What kind of impact can libraries have on individuals? How are** library services transforming people's lives? The transformative power of libraries requires the ability of those working in libraries to spark curiosity in themselves and others. The magic of transformation is using life to grow up, make wise decisions, and explore our potential. At their best, libraries can help people transform from childhood to adulthood, and adults to transform into greater maturity and self-mastery. How can librarians help themselves and others to develop skills, learn to think, and enact principled ideals?

Over a century ago, Helen Keller, author, lecturer, and the first deaf-blind person to receive a college degree, wrote, "As my college days draw to a close, I find myself looking forward with beating heart and bright anticipations to what the future holds of activity for me. My share in the work of the world may be limited; but the fact that it is work makes it precious. Nay, the desire and will to work is optimism itself."[1]

Today's technology—or digital media or new media or digital technology—gives us unprecedented capacity for exploring information and ideas, creating individually or with others, and connecting with people near and far. The wise use of new and emerging technologies is "optimism itself."

To take advantage of these new tools for learning, developing the mind, and expanding our ability to cooperate and get things done, we need to discover both good and bad effects of technology. How can librarians maintain an optimistic outlook as we grapple with the breathtaking pace and rapid changes in technology? How can we live with budget uncertainties, yet be compelled to take risks to improve services?

Technology strengthens the ability of the library to fulfill its purpose to help enlighten humanity, such as offering services to download free electronic books to handheld devices to read, think, and explore ideas at your fingertips. Technology will not drive libraries out of business, unless we don't ask the right questions and think things through.

Lisa Guernsey, director of the Learning Technologies Project and director of Early Ed Initiative at New America, writes, "The daily lives of children and their families' routines are now shaped by what they watch and when, and how they interact with [technologies]."[2] Guernsey speaks eloquently about the factors parents, educators, and librarians need to take into account for children to benefit from technology, her three C's: "the *content* on the screen, the *context* of use, and the age and characteristics of each individual *child*."[3] Libraries can take that a step further by supporting children, teens, and adults to make wise decisions about content and context, and how to pursue their own interests to benefit all.

A library that sparks curiosity becomes a shaper of maturity and character for children and adults. By putting potentially transforming experiences—including emerging technologies—into people's lives, libraries can offer valuable opportunities. By making a long-term commitment to mentor individuals of all ages to stimulate their thinking, libraries can become extraordinary, even magical, places.

Libraries are using more new and emerging technologies and incorporating them into programs and services. How can we take things up several notches to embrace a new future for libraries? Years from now, will libraries even be called libraries? How can we serve the community despite the financial challenges and the closed-minded attitudes toward technology of a portion of those working in and using libraries?

Librarians can stay optimistic, without ignoring technological challenges and funding restraints. How can we steadily progress and bring out what Plato described as the "good" in our community, despite the problems of society? Helen Keller answered this question: "I am never discouraged by absence of good. I never can be argued into hopelessness. Doubt and mistrust are the mere panic of timid imagination, which the steadfast heart will conquer, and the large mind transcend."[4]

# MAKE TECHNOLOGY AND LEARNING FUN AND PRACTICAL

Many libraries are transforming sections of their physical space into STEM (science, technology, engineering, math) labs, innovation labs, exploration points, play spots, play-and-learn centers, and makerspaces—using new technologies alongside traditional methods to enjoy learning. Sewing machines can be seen next to 3-D printers. Board games, such as Monopoly, are next to computer stations devoted to online games. These places are keeping in mind the need "to be sure technology and media do not displace active play, time outdoors, hands-on activities with real materials, and creative expression through art, music, and movement,"[5] as Chip Donohue, dean of Distance Learning and Continuing Education, and director of TEC Center, Erikson Institute, writes.

"Recently I was sitting in the Children's Room watching a nine-year-old boy teach his grandmother how to play Minecraft [an online game with creative and building aspects allowing players to build constructions out of textured cubes in a 3-D procedurally generated world]," says Amanda Courie, youth services coordinator, Caroline County (MD) Library. "They were building a birchwood house together, and suddenly came across some squid! She was open and curious. I could see how much the grandson enjoyed being the expert and giving his grandmother a glimpse into a world in which he is right at home."

Carisa Kluver, founder of the app review site Digital-Storytime.com, adds, "Librarians have a daily opportunity to model how families can turn computer devices—an otherwise solitary experience—into engaging and interactive learning tools to be shared between adults and children."

When it comes to inspiring people to take advantage of emerging technology, gadgets, computer coding, 3-D printing, creative electrical circuitry—what better place than a library! When it comes to stimulating curiosity about technology and many other areas of life in order to expand and improve ourselves as human beings—what better place than a library! Libraries can attract the resources to offer a wide array of fun technology and other creativity tools to help develop young and old minds alike.

One of the purposes-within-the-purpose of a library can be making technology enjoyable to spark curiosity. A key approach in fulfilling this purpose is the idea of library staff mentoring adults, teens, and children. Librarians can support parents and caregivers to make the healthiest media decisions for their family, and to successfully guide children through the changing landscape of digital media and technology.

Dr. Susan B. Neuman and Dr. Donna C. Celano, authors of *Giving Our Children a Fighting Chance: Poverty, Literacy, and the Development of Information Capital*, describe how libraries can take on new roles and responsibilities. They write: "If libraries are to provide equal access to resources for all our citizens, we must consider . . . [point-of-need] training [and mentoring] that strategically provide information navigation skills to adults and their young children to promote higher quality uses of the library resources."[6]

Neuman and Celano observed library services in action for over ten years. Their research conclusions demonstrated that many parents believe a strong self-teaching aspect is part of new technologies, and therefore their role as first teacher is less important when using these digital tools. In addition, many parents may be intimidated by new and emerging technologies. This scenario catapults librarians into naturally becoming media mentors. This mentoring role, and other changing roles, are part of what many people call "the new librarian." The new librarian stimulates curiosity, offers fun tech opportunities, and connects and collaborates with people so that individuals, families, businesses, and organizations can make the best decisions possible as they learn, grow, and contribute to the community.

Lisa Guernsey has put out a call to action for children's librarians to take on this new role: become media mentors for parents and children. Mentoring children means planting a seed and nurturing it as they grow into adults. Mentoring and

An example of a Squishy Circuit to explore electrical conductivity. Carroll County (MD) Public Library.

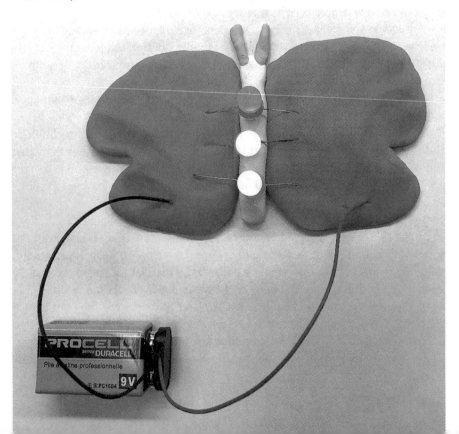

supporting parents and caregivers can help adults think through media decisions for themselves and their children.

Let's expand this idea in four ways. First, enlist all library staff (not just children's librarians) to get busy becoming effective media mentors to people of all ages. Second, develop our minds to think and ask, what more can I learn to be successful in my mentor role? Third, collaborate with adults in the community—such as engineers, small business owners, philosophers, and even beekeepers—to mentor teens and older youth to mentor children. And fourth, make a long-term commitment for your library to provide digital media, technology, and other kinds of information mentorship. In these ways, the new librarian can be instrumental in offering the kinds of opportunities and experiences that can transform individual lives and increase the vitality of a community.

Can one positive library experience encourage a parent to come back regularly or change her attitude toward learning? Yes! Can a series of fun tech programs motivate a failing, pessimistic teen into a top-of-the-class scholar and optimist? Absolutely yes! Can you live with the fact that you may or may not be aware of these kinds of changes and results?

Some naysayers may scoff at the idea that people are capable of transforming their lives—that any one of us can increase our skills and talents at any point in life and under any circumstances. Let's take a look at a remarkable and inspiring story.

Helen Keller lost her eyesight and hearing at nineteen months after experiencing a high fever. She changed from a cheerful toddler to a child filled with anger, frustration, and pessimism. By the time she was six years old, Helen's parents were desperate to help their daughter.

Mrs. Keller read an inspiring account about an educated deaf-blind girl, Laura Bridgman, in *American Notes* by Charles Dickens. She tried to contact the doctor who worked with Bridgman only to discover that he died. The Kellers' local physician suggested visiting a Dr. Chisholm in Baltimore. The family took the long train journey from their home in Alabama in 1886 to meet with Dr. Chisholm. He was unable to help but arranged for the Kellers to meet with Alexander Graham Bell in Washington DC.

Bell, who was famous for his pioneering work with the telephone, spent much of his life helping deaf people, teaching ways to communicate and designing hearing devices. Helen dedicated her autobiography to Bell and writes, "Child as I was, I at once felt the tenderness and sympathy which endeared Dr. Bell to so many hearts. . . . He understood my signs, and I knew it and loved him at once. But I did not dream that that interview would be the door through which I would pass from darkness into light, from isolation into friendship, companionship, knowledge, love."[7] Dr. Bell connected the Kellers to the Perkins School for the Blind in Boston. Through Perkins, Anne Sullivan, an instructor and visually impaired herself, was asked to take on the role of governess to Helen Keller.

Anne Sullivan was only twenty when she began working with six-year-old Helen in 1887. It was the start of a nearly fifty-year mentorship and friendship.

Anne made learning and technology enjoyable for Helen—that is, the technology of their time, such as objects, books in braille, and the typewriter. Anne helped Helen spark her curiosity. Helen not only learned to communicate with others but to read—and read widely—and to write. Helen went on to graduate from Radcliffe College at Harvard University. She dedicated herself to causes such as the American Foundation for the Blind, and became a surprisingly active and productive person and prolific writer. She continues inspiring people around the world who hear of her and read her books.

Helen Keller and Anne Sullivan, Cape Cod, MA, July 1888.

Research shows that teens are often drawn to the library to explore new technology, to use computers, and to relax, learn, and socialize with peers.[8] Many teens have demonstrated a willingness to participate—formally and informally—as a mentee and as a mentor, especially when it comes to learning and using new technologies. As Sullivan and Keller demonstrated, mentoring is a long-term commitment.

A position paper on media mentorship by the Association for Library Service to Children (ALSC) observes: "Libraries have the capacity to support families with all their literacy needs, traditional and digital, including needs as they arise . . . This role as media mentor is a core function of supporting the lives . . . of children and families [for years to come]."[9] This long-term commitment to spark curiosity and to make learning and technology enjoyable is central to a library's success. This kind of commitment can create transformational experiences for individuals and families—and can help make a library a magical destination in any community.

Questions and points to ponder:

1. How can librarians help themselves and others to develop skills, learn to think, and express principled ideals?
2. How can we promote the wise use of new and emerging technology as "optimism itself"?

3. How can we serve the community despite the financial challenges and the closed-minded attitudes toward technology of a portion of those working in and using libraries?

4. The definition—and magic—of the new librarian is one who stimulates curiosity, offers fun tech opportunities, and connects and collaborates with people, so that individuals, families, businesses, and organizations can make the best decisions possible as they learn, grow, and contribute to the community. How can I stimulate curiosity in myself and others?

## Notes

1. Helen Keller, *Optimism.* (1903; Marble Hill, GA: Enthea Press, 2006), 29.
2. Lisa Guernsey, *New America: Education Policy Program Policy Brief: Envisioning a Digital Age Architecture for Early Education.* (March 2014), 2–3.
3. Ibid.
4. Keller, *Optimism,* 28–29.
5. Chip Donohue, chap. 3 of *Technology and Digital Media in the Early Years: Tools for Teaching and Learning* (New York: Routledge and NAEYC, 2015), 21.
6. Susan Neuman and Donna C. Celano, *Giving Our Children a Fighting Chance: Poverty, Literacy, and the Development of Information Capital* (New York: Teachers College Press, 2012), 128.
7. Helen Keller, *The Story of My Life* (1903; New York: Bantam Classic, 2005), 13.
8. Linda W. Braun, Maureen L. Hartman, Sandra Hughes-Hassell, and Kafi Kumasi, with contributions from Beth Yoke on behalf of the Young Adult Library Services Association, *The Future of Library Services for and with Teens: A Call to Action* (Chicago: ALA/YALSA 2014), 1.
9. Cen Campbell, Claudia Haines, Amy Koester, and Dorothy Stoltz, on behalf of the Association for Library Service to Children (ALSC), *Media Mentorship in Libraries Serving Youth,* 2015, 1, 9.

# 15

# EVERYDAY EFFORTS, EVERYDAY GREATNESS

*The challenge for us is not to wipe out our past history but to learn to live together in the future.*
**—ANDREW YOUNG, CIVIL RIGHTS ADVOCATE**

**Working with others is like listening to a great symphony or** concerto. Structured from the eighteenth-century opera sinfonia, a symphony contains multiple distinct sections: a fast movement, a slow movement, and a dance-like movement. A collaborative effort can have distinct characteristics too: ups and downs, slow and fast pacing, a time for a quick rhythm baroque dance or bourrée, and a time for a slow waltz. It will likely have a wide range of tempo similar to classical music, from Rossini's *William Tell* overture (a great chase-scene theme used in the movie and TV show *The Lone Ranger*) to Brahms's *Hungarian Dance No. 5* (a lively dance tune) to the second movement from the *Clarinet Concerto in A Major* by Mozart (to be played adagio, or slowly).

Like an orchestra, a high-performing community team is able to work in harmony despite the need for counterpoint or interweaving separate melodies. This team of everyday greatness creates synergy to implement its common mission and activities. It honors contributions made by all—the library, the school, the health department, the small business, the local bank, and the neighborhood church. Cross-rhythms can be handled as long as the pitch is the same. When a theme is agreed upon (such as school readiness, technology skill development, or reading for fun) musical notes can be assigned for each instrument. An everyday great team doesn't try to "go to scale" in the sense that bigger is always better, but it uses the notes and melodies on the scale to step up to use best practices. Its rhythm between movements will be modulated by involving a pivotal common chord (such as a kindergarten assessment, fun tech devices, or a reading contest). From time to time a brief, often showy solo of improvisatory character—perhaps a local research study, a state award, or front-page newspaper coverage—will help herald in the next movement. In time, the collaborative team will produce an everyday masterpiece.

In order to achieve everyday greatness in a library, no matter the size of staff, budget, or community, you need to plan for it. This kind of planning, however, is behind the scenes and invisible to most observers. Staying above the fray, thinking things through, and sparking curiosity can help you plan effectively each day. "Soft skills" or everyday virtues, such as resilience, patience, humor, goodwill, and integrity, give you the ability to plan and implement successfully. They are examples of practical efforts to create everyday greatness in libraries. Behind-the-scenes planning goes along with the idea of how an orchestra can learn to play together to produce a beautiful symphony.

In 1924, Helen Keller wrote to the New York Symphony Orchestra about her experience "listening" on the radio to their performance of Beethoven's *Ninth Symphony* as a deaf-blind person.

> Last night, when the family was listening to your wonderful rendering of the immortal symphony someone suggested that I put my hand on the receiver and see if I could get any of the vibrations . . . The intertwined and intermingling vibrations from different instruments enchanted me. I could actually distinguish the cornets, the roll of the drums, deep-toned violas and violins singing in exquisite unison . . . When the human voices leaped up thrilling from the surge of harmony, I recognized them instantly as voices more ecstatic, upcurving swift and flame-like, until my heart almost stood still . . . As I listened, with darkness and melody, shadow and sound filling all the room, I could not help remembering that the great composer who poured forth such a flood of sweetness into the world was deaf like myself. I marveled at the power of his quenchless spirit by which out of his pain he wrought such joy for others—and there I sat, feeling with my hand the magnificent symphony which broke like a sea upon the silent shores of his soul and mine.[1]

Many of the fruits of collaboration are inaudible or invisible. Yet these intangibles are essential in supporting community life. To encourage a great collaboration, we must create an everyday ambience through those we hire, the programs and services we offer, and the collections we develop. Libraries need workers with compassion and the ability to spark curiosity in themselves and others. Library programs and services should inspire people to think, create, and contribute to society. Access to great books and information offers the opportunity for everyone in a community to explore ideas, pursue being their best, and give voice to their contributions.

Beethoven wrote *Symphony No. 9 in D Minor* one hundred years before Helen Keller experienced its joy. It was the first major symphony to use voices. Also known as "The Choral," the composition uses four voices and a chorus in the final movement. The words were taken from a poem written by Friedrich Schiller called "Ode to Joy":

> Joy is the name of the strong spring
> In eternal nature.
> Joy, joy drives the wheels
> In the great clock of worlds.

Schiller, eighteenth-century German philosopher, playwright, and poet, described joy as the means to creativity and higher-level thinking. Wedding the good with the beautiful and cultivating our sensitivity for both—by cultivating the best within us and the best within the world—we do not become slaves to the dark side of nature and do not squander "our citizenship in the intelligible world."[2] How can we avoid becoming a slave to negativity especially in the midst of a challenge? How can we wed the best skills and splendor of our fellow human beings in our collaborative efforts despite facing difficulties?

The library can be an uplifting spirit in a community and a great source of celebration. "Librarians can focus on transformative services that proactively address barriers to success," says Denise Davis, Cecil County (MD) Public Library director. "We can enhance services such as school readiness and career-oriented lifelong learning, and not limit our focus to transactions, like circulation of books and storytime attendance. We can concentrate our talents and skills to close the opportunity gap for users, providing pivotal services, resources, and experiences, and prove value by showing transformations."

She adds, "One of our roles is to be problem-solvers. For example, what is holding someone back as an entrepreneur, how can the library support small business? How can we get books and summer educational activities to more children, including lower-income kids who may lack transportation, to deter summer learning decline and that research shows can be averted by visiting public libraries? How can we learn more to educate, engage, and inspire our users in achieving their goals and dreams?"

# USE ADVERSITY TO YOUR ADVANTAGE

Maryland libraries and others across the country introduced the concept of a "learning organization" as a strategy to turn a problem into a challenge. At the heart of this strategy was the idea that "we're each responsible for our own learning." In 1995–97, Carroll County (MD) Public Library underwent reorganization, created a team approach to better fulfill the library's purpose, and embraced "a learning culture that inspires employees to achieve excellence leading to a passion for internal and external customer service. The role of all library staff in this culture is to embody innovation, creativity, learning, and risk taking in an atmosphere of respect, support, and trust. Employees will seek challenges, intellectual stimulation, and venture into the realm of curiosity to do ambitious work in a fun workplace."[3]

Today many recent Carroll library employees may not necessarily realize this history or use the "learning organization" terms, such as systems thinking and personal mastery; yet the learning philosophy is practiced daily because it's stamped into the culture. The culture of learning and growing involves "an individual's personal responsibility for lifelong learning in support of the advancement of system goals and priorities. It is understood that we all need to be teachers [and mentors] as well as learners."[4] Staff seek out new ideas and new technology, and listen to the community using a proactive stance to improve customer service. Results have shown that Carroll is a busy library with one of the highest circulations of library materials per capita in the state for over twenty years. Carroll's programs, activities, and events are a strategic plan priority resulting as a library with one of the highest number of programs offered statewide.

How have libraries used the challenges of the last twenty-five years to our benefit? How have we disregarded the naysayers who declare that libraries will become irrelevant? "We want people to walk into a library not only to find books but to access digital technologies, to participate in enriching conversations and experiences, and to expand their minds," explains John Bertot, a professor at University of Maryland's iSchool. In the mid-1990s with the advent of the Internet, many libraries grappled with finding ways to capitalize on that new and exciting information resource. With the development of electronic ink and the first Kindle reading device in 2007, reading long passages on a computer tablet became easier on the eye. In 2008, the economic downturn hit many communities, creating tough choices about library services. The invention of touchscreen technology with the iPad in 2010 was a milestone, along with now more affordable fun technologies such as 3-D printing and "squishy" electrical circuitry.

Carroll County's kindergarten assessment demonstrates how a library can join forces with community partners to step up to a challenge. It demonstrates how effective it can be to renew a plan and to re-harness the energy of a team. In the

Making the Enoch Pratt Free Library, Baltimore, MD, exciting for families with a Fairy Tale Extravaganza, reading to dogs, making a 3-D printed bracelet, and honoring a native literary favorite, Edgar Allan Poe.

first years of the assessment known as the Maryland Model for School Readiness, 2001–09, the county ranked as low as 19 out of 24 jurisdictions. The early learning community outreach division of the school system, known as the Judy Center, stepped up to lead the effort. "Early childhood consortium members worked together to enhance the role of each individual agency in order to better support parents in their role as first teacher. Increased communication among partners was essential," says Joyce Tierney, director for the Family Center, Human Services Programs, and cochair of the consortium.

The library successfully conducted a research-tested study to determine the effectiveness of its training of home child-care providers on children's early literacy skills.[5] Strategies include cross-training agency staff on early childhood development and school readiness. A pool of parent educators in several agencies is charged with conducting home visitations using the Parents as Teachers (PAT) curriculum.[6] Thirteen hours per week of a library staff member are devoted to using PAT during home child-care provider visits. The Every Child Ready to Read @ your library toolkit helped structure outreach efforts to families who don't use the library.[7] Closer communication between early childhood educators and kindergarten teachers, as well as offering more resources through the library, added important elements to the effort.

The library participates on several levels in the consortium—for example, enhancing early literacy skill development and parent knowledge in storytimes, creating school readiness kits for parents and caregivers to borrow, and developing an outstanding collection of children's books. Library staff members reach out to child-care settings and schools through bookmobile services; maintain dynamic play-and-learn centers in each branch; conduct learning parties; and offer early childhood education trainings with credit hours. Every Child Ready to Read's five practices—talking, singing, reading, writing, and playing—and its research-based

Carroll County (MD) Early Childhood Consortium.

Patron Lindsay Edwards (Westminster Branch, Carroll County (MD) Public Library) says, "I will treasure my weekly routine of visiting the play-and-learn area with my two boys . . . The [imaginative play setting and toys are] unlike what we could ever have at home."

*Photo by Stephanie Zinger.*

content are infused into all aspects of programs, collections, and family-friendly spaces, as well as parent workshops, library café discussion programs, and early learning activities inside and outside the library. Symbolically, the five practices are available as posters for partners to hang on the walls in their settings. As of this writing, Carroll's kindergarten assessment scores have ranked first or second in the state since 2009–10, generally with 95 percent of children ready for school.

## Uplift the Quality of Human Life

Enoch Pratt, American businessman and philanthropist, was admired by Andrew Carnegie. In fact, Pratt's gift of $1 million to create a free lending library in 1882 in the city of Baltimore—a central library and four branches—became a model for Carnegie's library grant program to build more than 1,600 American libraries from 1889 to 1919. Enoch Pratt envisioned that his library would be free "for all."[8] "For fifteen years, I have studied the library question, and wondered what I could do with my money so that it would do the most good," he explained. "I soon made up my mind that I would not found a college—for a few rich. My library shall be for all, rich and poor without distinction of race or color, who, when properly accredited, can take out the books if they will handle them carefully and return them."[9]

In 1905, Carnegie donated $500,000 to build twenty additional Pratt library branches in Baltimore. The Enoch Pratt Free Library became one of the most reputable organizations in the country known for exceptional library service. Today the central library houses an outstanding state library resource center. Regional libraries, neighborhood branches, and bookmobiles round out the organization. In 2010, library visits increased to more than two million—a 58 percent increase in two years, topping attendance of the city's Ravens football games. Enoch Pratt Free Library's director, Dr. Carla Hayden, says the upcoming 2015–18 renovation of the

Pratt sat on the board of the Peabody Institute music conservatory in Baltimore only a few decades after Beethoven completed his *Ninth Symphony*. We can imagine the robust final movement inspiring Pratt and others to be motivated to serve their community and to donate money to establish the music conservatory on Mount Vernon Place, the Walters Art Museum across the street, Johns Hopkins University uptown and hospital across town, and the first "free" lending public library on 400 Cathedral Street, Baltimore.

central library "will not change what works well in the building, such as our school readiness efforts, teen programming, great collection, and popular computer access, but will create a dynamic new space for all ages to enjoy for generations to come."

Ponder these points and questions about overcoming adversity and striving for everyday greatness.

1. To encourage a great collaboration, how can I get in tune with the intangibles to uplift human life and create an everyday ambience through those I hire, the programs and services I offer, and the collections my library develops? What are these intangibles?
2. How can I use the challenges of the last twenty-five years (or ten years, or five years) to my library's benefit? What strategies do I have to disregard the naysayers who declare that libraries will become irrelevant?
3. Since growth means progression directed forward and upward, how can I uplift the quality of human life in practical ways in my job at the library? What can my library do to support the growth of my community?
4. How is my role in my library organization or my role in a community collaboration like a bassoon player or violinist in an orchestra? How about comparing my role to the conductor of the orchestra?

## Notes

1. *The Auricle* 2, no. 6 (March 1924). American Foundation for the Blind, Helen Keller Archives, accessed July 2015, www.afb.org.

2. Adapted from Dorothy Stoltz, Marisa Conner, and James Bradberry, *The Power of Play: Designing Early Learning Spaces* (Chicago: ALA Editions, 2015), 7; from Frederich Schiller, "On the Sublime," accessed July 2015, www.schillerinstitute.org/transl/trans_on_sublime.html_www.schillerinstitute.org; and Friedrich Schiller, "Ode to Joy," trans. Wikisource, accessed July 2015, https://en.wikisource.org/wiki/Ode_to_Joy.

3. Taken from Carroll County (MD) Public Library Learning Philosophy.

4. Ibid.

5. Elaine Czarnecki, *A Report: Carroll County Public Library Emergency Literacy Assessment Training Project*, http://library.carr.org/about/docs/emlitreport.pdf.

6. Parents as Teachers, www.parentsasteachers.org.

7. Every Child Ready to Read @ your library (http://everychildreadytoread.org/) is a joint initiative of the Association of Library Service to Children (ALSC) and Public Library Association (PLA).

8. "Enoch Pratt Free Library—Central Branch," *Explore Baltimore Heritage*, accessed July 2015, http://explore.baltimoreheritage.org/items/show/41#.VZmU41KULRs.

9. Kari Barbic, "Enoch Pratt," Philanthropic Roundtable, accessed July 2015, www.philanthropyroundtable.org/almanac/hall_of_fame/enoch_pratt.

# 16

# INSPIRING YOUR COMMUNITY

*The force of character is cumulative.*
—RALPH WALDO EMERSON

██████████ **In recent years, library work has increasingly become community** collaborative work, in which a library plans with schools, businesses, and organizations to support common activities. These collaborations produce programs and services that enrich the community far beyond what an individual person could accomplish. How can library staff establish relationships with school personnel, business owners, organization representatives, and other community leaders to cooperate on joint projects—and together build what some would call "community character"?

An excellent model for a strong collaborative effort was the tie between Britain and the United States during World War II. Even if you are not particularly fond of history, this example can offer timeless wisdom about cooperation. It was based on a long and close liaison between Winston Churchill, prime minister of Great Britain, and Franklin Delano Roosevelt, president of the United States.

Their collaboration started with a moment of serendipity in 1918 at the end of the First World War. The much younger Roosevelt and Churchill met briefly when Roosevelt was visiting England as assistant secretary of the US Navy. In less than friendly circumstances Churchill—then minister of British munitions—expressed frustration about how the United States remained neutral in the war from 1914 to 1917, alienating Roosevelt and other Americans at a dinner.

In the early '30s, when Roosevelt became US president, Churchill reached out by sending an amiable message to the president through Roosevelt's son, who was visiting London. In 1939 at the outbreak of World War II, Churchill was appointed first lord of the Admiralty. Roosevelt sent him a telegram asking to be kept directly apprised of British naval developments. Few would have foreseen that less than a year later, Churchill—who spent much of the 1920s and '30s as a political outcast—would be prime minister, leading England against despotism.

The two men communicated on more than 1,700 occasions and spent 120 days together in meetings during the war in Washington DC, Hyde Park, New York, and several other places around the world. Franklin's wife, Eleanor, described how Roosevelt and Churchill had "a good understanding of each other and an ability to work together easily." The men found they had enough in common—a love of history, the navy, books, and other literary interests—to "enjoy each other's company."

Eleanor gave an example of their camaraderie in an article for *The Atlantic* in 1965. She told the story about the three of them traveling together by car to Shangri-La, a presidential retreat not far from DC, now Camp David. They drove through Frederick, Maryland. Franklin pointed out the historic house of Barbara Fritchie, who at age ninety-five waved the Union flag to antagonize the Confederate troops marching through town. Churchill launched into the 1864 poem about Fritchie, reciting it in its entirety. "My husband and I looked at each other, for each of us could have quoted a few lines, but the whole was quite beyond us! Franklin happened to be fond of Edward Lear's *Nonsense Rhymes*, and I can remember Mr. Churchill capping every rhyme my husband quoted. How long they could have gone on, I don't know, but fortunately a turn in the road brought an end to this particular amusement."[1]

How do leaders bring out the best in each other's character in order to better serve the community? How do people throughout a library organization create a robust liaison with the people in a partner organization?

DISCOVERY #16

# CREATE A CORE OF STRENGTH AND GENEROSITY

To be a successful community partner, library staff members need to muster a positive approach in their thoughts and actions—even when facing challenges or disagreements. They can develop a core of strength (thinking skills, courage, optimism, and curiosity) and a core of generosity (helpfulness, compassion, and a big-picture view of community connections). The more we learn to "lead an examined life," as Socrates encouraged, by taking time to reflect on our collaborative work, the more we can find ways to rejuvenate regularly in order to respond appropriately and prioritize quickly. We should take time to reinvigorate our energy and resources in smart and useful ways before we get burned out.

"It's important to focus on finding out what is important to your community," says Mary Hastler, CEO of Harford County (MD) Public Library and president of the Maryland Library Association. "Rather than focusing solely on your goal, get to know what is going on in the lives of others. It's not so much about what the library offers as it is about what people need."

Of course, figuring out what your customers or patrons need is the challenge. There lies the heart of collaboration. It's not always a good idea to give people what they want; we should help people go beyond what they *want* by satisfying what they *need*. In that way, they will come back to the library again and again.

What might satisfying a need look like? As a hypothetical example, a thirteen-year-old grudgingly goes to a library's "farm to fork" event with his parents and by chance listens to a chef describe how to prepare a healthy dish. The teen never would have sought out the program as something he would *want* to do, but stumbled upon the opportunity created by the lecture. He discovers an insatiable curiosity in himself for cooking that leads him to sign up for his regional school district's culinary program. The library becomes a regular source for information, stimulation, and motivation in his life by checking out numerous cookbooks, making useful recommendations for new titles, and creating social connections at library programs. Through attending business-planning classes at the library and getting support from librarians to do market research and use the library's sophisticated business-focused databases, at age twenty-one, he opens a small restaurant in town. He becomes a community partner offering sponsorships to support summer reading, and is a local favorite giving regular lectures at the library—and, of course, its annual "farm to fork" event. This now young chef and business owner joins the library's fundraising committee and creates a young-professionals group dedicated to raising awareness of and money for the public library.

Hastler said in a broadcast interview, "The more we as librarians can be part of their world, the more our partners help us shape library services to be responsive to the community."[2] In one example, Hastler and her staff aspired to develop a collection of superhero dolls (such as Spider-Man and Wolverine) and related books as circulating kits. They did not have the extra money in library operating funds. In a conversation with a Walmart representative, however, at a chamber of commerce breakfast, Hastler expressed her support of a new store, knowing how valuable it would be to the people in that area. Her main message was: we want to support your business because we care about what's going on in our community. To her surprise, the library foundation received a call from the store offering funds to sponsor the summer reading program, and Walmart was thrilled to be offered the opportunity to sponsor the Super Hero Collection as an alternative.

Captain America circulating kit. Harford County (MD) Public Library.

The program, intended to help engage all young readers, invites students to check out an action figure and then write and record their "adventures" in a notebook in the kit. The next students then write their own stories in the notebook. The program is intended to help students read, play, interact, and develop their writing skills. On the first day of Summer Reading 2015, the kits hit library branch shelves; children quickly discovered them and checked out the entire branch collection of seventy-five kits within sixty minutes.

In two other Harford examples, an early learning center funded a "Little Leapers" science kit collection for all the branches, and a local bank donated money to support digital-media activities in an innovation lab at the Abington Branch.

Kerol Harrod, youth librarian, Denton Public Library, and coeditor of several professional books, including *Marketing Your Library*, says, "We asked ourselves, how can the library connect more to the community and help children learn about their community and about the importance of reading." This question led Kerol to create, write, and coproduce the award-winning children's television show *Library Larry's Big Day*. The monthly television show aired from 2010 to 2015 and highlighted organizations and businesses in the city and county of Denton, Texas. The show featured three puppet characters: Library Larry, a Texas bull, Mr. Chompers, a jolly hippo, and Emmy Lou Dickenson, a word-loving pig whose name reveres American poet Emily Dickinson.

Each episode was upbeat and funny, and took children on a tour to places around the county, such as a brick-making plant, heritage center, a municipal court, and the airport, introducing vocabulary words like *manufacture* and *propeller*. An especially big day was visiting the George W. Bush Presidential Library and Museum. Terri Gibbs, the city's director of libraries, said the show brought "civic literacy to a local level. It offered children a glimpse into the community around them . . . The humor was such that I think it appealed to all ages."

The library decided to sunset *Library Larry's Big Day* television show while it was still on top. The five-year outreach initiative, produced by the Denton Public Library and Denton Television in association with the Denton Independent School District, accomplished many collaboration goals and promoted early literacy. The show received numerous awards and accolades, including the "Best Regularly Scheduled Television Program" from the City-County Communications & Marketing Association, the leading national organization for government communications. The library mobilized enough talent and strength and gave generously of its time and resources in those five years to create a remarkable level of community goodwill. Denton Public Library is now experimenting with other ways to connect to families who don't use the library, by setting up a booth and bringing storytime activities to one of their many community partners visited by Library Larry: the farmers' market.

## Tapping the Best within Ourselves and Others

Barbara Squires, director of Leadership Development at the Annie E. Casey Foundation and former assistant commissioner at the Baltimore City Health Department,

Honoring local sponsorships for an innovation lab. Harford County (MD) Public Library.
*(J. Thomas Photography)*

describes the process of bringing out the best in each other as individuals and organizations: "When the Leadership in Action Program (LAP) was created state-wide in Maryland in the early 2000s, we were expected through the leadership program to work together toward a *specific result*, not to work better in a general way. Statewide we focused on school readiness. We had the data to go along with it because the state department of education created a kindergarten assessment. The *data* told us why we were at the table together—to increase school readiness."

The cross-section nature of the LAP collaboration meant that by virtue of the work each partner did, the health department and each agency had a part in supporting families to help their children get ready for school. They had a key mantra: "What more can we do?" The collaborative effort pushed each person and each organization to ask: Is there more we can be doing to accelerate results? The Health Department, for example, already focused on a number of child health indicators, but they asked, "What more can we do?" They looked at their home nurse visitation program and pondered, "Can we do more with this program?"

At the same time, Ellen Riordan at the Pratt Library asked her colleagues, what more could they do. The library created a "First Card" service where parents sign up their baby for a library card and can check out books for their family. They revamped a bookmobile to become a Book Buggy, focused on early literacy. The Book Buggy reaches out to families, such as those visiting federally funded food and nutrition programs or Women, Infants, and Children (WIC) centers run by the health department. Squires's home-visiting nurses at the Health Department were then trained to distribute early literacy information and help the library sign up families for baby's "First Card."

Amazingly enough, these LAPs extended their time even after the grant funding ended. Squires explains, "The staying power of the LAPs said a lot to the value of these collaborations. I met lots of wonderful people and established long-term relationships. We learned together as a group the value of school readiness and that every agency plays a role. At the urging of the collaboration, we stretched ourselves to do more." Statewide school readiness improved remarkably. Squires adds, "I'm not sure I'd have made the leap into early childhood in such a big way without the collaboration. I can now pick up the phone and call a partner, knowing that I can easily get that person's buy-in for a project because he or she understands the issues. It's less about finding funding to do something and more about working together toward specific results."

Joint planning and decision making can bring out the best in each partner. The World War II partnership between the United States and Great Britain was successful in large part because Churchill and Roosevelt were highly motivated to collaborate and take action. "People at the top must support the collaboration.

Anyone in an organization can start a collaboration, but to be successful in the long run, leadership's full support is needed," says Nancy Bolt, library consultant, author, and former state librarian of Colorado. A leader's interest and support set a tone for the whole organization.

Sarah Mackey, Ready to Read Corps, Columbus (OH) Metropolitan Library, says, "We made great strides in our home visitation program after the CEO of the library and the CEO of the hospital agreed to up the ante by sharing information in a way to more fully support each other." The hospital wanted to give literacy and school-readiness information and opportunities to the at-risk, poor families who are their patients. The library wanted to be a resource of literacy and school readiness for poor families whose children may be at risk of not being on track for kindergarten. One of the outstanding results of leader-to-leader correspondence was the agreement for the hospital to share patient-contact information giving the library the ability to directly contact families to offer Ready to Read Corps visits.

The Columbus library won a 2011 National Medal for Museum and Library Service award for services including Ready to Read Corps. Sarah explains, "We are now reaching families we don't usually see coming into our libraries. Through a formal evaluation we did with Ohio State University, we know that Ready to Read Corps helps parental attitudes towards encouraging learning for themselves and their children. Children's preliteracy knowledge increased an amazing 25 percent in the first twelve months." The library is now serving more than 3,800 families who might not otherwise use the library.

## Learning from Great Leaders

Learning about great leaders is an object lesson that can help librarians—no matter the circumstances—develop core strengths and a spirit of generosity. We don't have to be the leader of the world or try to save the world, but can draw on the best within ourselves and the best in others to serve the community.

When Roosevelt died, Churchill explained that in part his admiration was due to President Roosevelt's physical handicap, which "lay heavily upon him. It was a marvel that he bore up against it [the effects of polio through the years] . . . not only in entering [the world] sphere, not only in acting vehemently in it, but in becoming indisputable master of the scene."[3]

In different ways, yet similar to his American counterpart, Churchill was an unlikely statesman. His story holds lessons for youth, such as how to use a difficult childhood to your benefit. Or how to seize all opportunities in order to learn to think for yourself. Or how to be a risk taker and use adversity to your advantage.

How to bolster success and put the inevitable failures behind you. And how to contribute your talents to the greater good with gusto and at the same time cultivate friendship, the ability to forgive, and dignity.

Winston Churchill was born two months premature and suffered from illness throughout his childhood, nearly dying of pneumonia at age ten. His parents were detached and unavailable. His father wrote him off as having no academic ability and encouraged Winston to go into the military. After the Boer War, Churchill experienced ups and downs in political life. He became a political scapegoat after the Chanak Crisis in Turkey in 1922 in which his party fell out of favor. During elections that year, running to stay in office as secretary of state for the colonies, his campaign was interrupted due to a sudden attack of appendicitis. He was defeated by more than ten thousand votes. He found himself, as he said, "without an office, without a seat, without a party, and even without an appendix." [4]

Struggling to keep himself above the fray and to make a living in the 1920s and '30s, Churchill became a prolific writer of history despite encounters with depression. He turned to landscape painting as a hobby and enjoyed the moral support of his wife, Clementine, during this challenging time—as well as throughout their long public life together and close marriage. Although a political outcast for nearly two decades, Churchill found ways to stay involved and to research world affairs through informed friends. He was one of the few to voice a strong and persistent warning against the rise of Hitler.

Without putting the greats like Churchill, Roosevelt, Helen Keller, and Benjamin Franklin on too high of a pedestal, we can learn from them. They are larger-than-life models for tapping the best within ourselves and others. They faced challenges and difficulties, just as everyone does. We can use them as examples of how we can lead and serve our communities through library work.

Like Churchill and Roosevelt, we can learn to forgive. They did not like each other when they met. Roosevelt was said to have called Churchill a "stinker" for bad-mouthing Americans near the end of World War I. They had to bury the hatchet before they could work together. You might not like some of the people in your collaboration or some of your library colleagues or staff members. It's not important to blame anyone for being a jerk. Forgive them and move on. Look at it as an opportunity to forgive that person and get along with him or her. If you fail to cooperate with someone in your community, it can mean missing a chance to do something for the greater good.

Collaboration means working together with not only those people or programs or businesses you like, but also with those you may not like. The American public library is at its best when the people who work in them take a neutral stance when it comes to politics and other issues. It doesn't matter whether an individual or

The Agape boys and their father enjoy a book together through Columbus (OH) Metropolitan Library's Ready to Read Corps.

local government or business is liberal or conservative or somewhere in the middle. Always remember the person you are serving is the person coming into the library, not your version of that person. Check your personal likes and dislikes in order to spark curiosity in the community one person at a time, no matter someone's race, religion, politics, or culinary tastes.

Some people don't like Walmart because it is big and allegedly takes advantage of people. Collaborating is not a time for self-indulgence (e.g., pious indignation), which, depending on the issue, can be easy for any of us to do from time to time. Instead, it is an opportunity to get to know people, get into the nitty-gritty of finding a common mission and activities, and work together to serve the community. When you develop relationships with people or community partners you don't initially like, you may be surprised by how much you actually have in common, how much you end up respecting them, and how much greater your impact can be in fulfilling community needs. You may end up like Churchill and Roosevelt, working hard, producing positive results, and all the while enjoying your colleague's company by reciting Edward Lear's *Nonsense Rhymes* together on a drive to your next meeting.

> The Goodnatured Grey Gull,
> carried the Old Owl, and his Crimson Carpet-bag,
> across the river, because he could not swim.[5]

Ponder the following points and questions about serving the community and how to be generous in thought and action.

1. How can I discover enough in common with my community colleagues to bring out their best skills and have what Eleanor Roosevelt described between her husband and Winston Churchill, "a good understanding of each other and an ability to work together easily"?
2. How can I bring out the best in someone's character in order to better serve the community? How can I create a robust liaison with the people in a partner organization?
3. How does learning about great leaders like Churchill and Roosevelt help me develop core strengths and a spirit of generosity?
4. As librarian Nancy Bolt points out, "People at the top must support the collaboration. Anyone in an organization can start a collaboration, but to be successful in the long run, leadership's full support is needed." What does this mean to me?
5. Forgiveness and collaboration go hand in hand in order to work together and be effective. How can I spark curiosity in the community one person at a time, no matter someone's race, religion, politics, or culinary tastes? Can I check my personal likes and dislikes, and recognize the person I am serving is the person coming into the library, not my version of that person?

## Notes

1. Eleanor Roosevelt, "Churchill at the White House," *Atlantic,* March 1965, www .theatlantic.com/magazine/archive/1965/03/churchill-at-the-white-house/305459/.
2. Mary Hastler, "Midday with Dan Rodricks," interview by Rodricks on WYPR radio, Baltimore, July 8, 2015.
3. "The Greatest Champion of Freedom," speech to the House of Commons (April 17, 1945), The Churchill Society, London, accessed July 2015, www.churchill-society -london.org.uk/DthRovlt.html.
4. Herbert G. Nicholas, "Sir Winston Churchill," *Encyclopaedia Britannica,* last updated June 11, 2015, www.britannica.com/biography/Winston-Churchill/ During-World-War-I.
5. "Different Types of Poems You Should Know About," from MakeLiterature.com, reprinted on All Things Healing, accessed July 2015, www.allthingshealing.com/ Poetry-Therapy/Different-Types-of-Poems-You-Should-Know-About/11330# .VgxeXMtdHIU.

# 17

# CELEBRATING SUCCESS!

*Scatter joy!*
—RALPH WALDO EMERSON

**Celebrating is an American custom. People come together to work** and celebrate each other's creativity and successes—whether it's new technologies developed by the virtuosos of the high-tech companies in Silicon Valley or by innovative teens in a neighborhood library. Or teaching children thinking skills. Or like Benjamin Franklin's Junto, his professional club of like-minded artisans in Philadelphia, improving themselves as individuals in order to improve the community. When we celebrate our best skills and attributes—and the best in libraries—we lay the groundwork for the next level of insight and innovation. We are uplifted and rewarded with more opportunities and ideas. Through celebration we are more willing to experiment and better able to enrich the community.

As library professionals, we can harness the energy of celebration to help us promote our services:

» Every time a customer or patron comes into the library or uses an online service, it's an opportunity to celebrate. That person is helping shape what a library can offer. It's a mutual celebration—the library serves the individual to help develop his or her best skills and attributes, and the person helps the library to figure out how to be its best.

» Celebrate when an at-risk family discovers how the library can support their journey in life to become more self-reliant. Let's ponder what it means to be self-reliant or self-sufficient as a family—or as a library worker. It means depending on yourself to get things done, but it does not mean that you do it all by yourself. That's where collaboration fits into the work we do in libraries. At the same time, self-reliance is *not* self-absorption. It is striving to be our best in order to think things through to be effective and contribute to society.

» Celebrate the success of library plans to offer exceptional service and create a culture of listening and responding to people in the community. Let's rejoice in the rapid changes in digital media and technology. It's time to celebrate when interested folk show up to discuss a book. When a fifteen-year-old with a chip-on-her-shoulder attitude helps corral misbehaving children to settle down in the library—bring out the party hats.

» Celebrate for the utter joy of it!

» Even when a community faces hardship and even tragedy, it's important to celebrate what's working well in that community. In this way we draw on our talents, skills, and accomplishments—the best within us—to solve problems and meet challenges and become stronger. How do we celebrate in both good times and bad times? How do we make collaboration work on a daily basis?

It's important to celebrate what's working well. You don't really need something specific, however; you can celebrate just for the heck of it. Presume success! Celebrate new plans, or simply celebrate for the sake of celebrating. It'll get your creative juices going.

DISCOVERY #17

## TAP THE SPIRIT OF CELEBRATION

One of the first steps in reaping the benefits of collaboration is to lighten up. We can then think about and celebrate what we already have instead of yearning for circumstances to be different. By reflecting on the good things in our communities, it's easy to see all that we have to be grateful for. Nini Beegan, Organizational Learning & Innovation, Maryland Division of Library Development & Services, says,

"A big-picture focus—to delight in the communities we serve—gives librarians an extraordinary opportunity to create a baseline pillar of strength."

We don't want to count our chickens before they hatch, or count down until doomsday, or count on someone else to do our thinking for us. It's easy for all of us, from time to time, to count the things that are wrong in a community and focus on failures, mistakes, and sadness. We can shift this focus by figuring out a way to move to a point of strength. The real challenge is to download not just a positive attitude, but a consistent, quiet enthusiasm and curiosity about life. The goal is to think about the good, as Plato said, and count our blessings, our friends, our talents, our lessons learned, our resources—internal and external, and our community treasures—like the library!

"The secret to success in collaboration is for a library to say yes as much as possible," says Kendra Jones, Children's Librarian, Tacoma (WA) Public Library System. By getting into the habit of thinking, "Ummm, what are the possibilities here?" we catapult the library into the realm of exceptional customer service. Another secret to success is the ability to say no when necessary by applying discernment. A key element is to avoid a knee-jerk reaction of saying no before thinking things through. Saying yes as much as possible combined with saying no when necessary is a managerial tool to use and celebrate.

We want to recognize and praise our ability to use discernment and the ability to think things through. Let's grapple with solving problems using an asset-focused, strength-based model. Let's spark curiosity by raising awareness of our community's creative powers. We in libraries can connect people so they can—together—think about the good in their community and use that to produce helpful and meaningful results.

A reason to study and celebrate great leaders from the past is to learn how they solved problems and created success. This should not be an exercise in confirming opinions we already hold; that would just be closed-mindedness. We want open-mindedness. Benjamin Franklin and Andrew Carnegie are so important in libraries because without their efforts, libraries would not exist. This book about how libraries can plan effectively to collaborate successfully would not exist.

Franklin promoted the idea of a lending library; though membership dues were required, it was the first library open to the public and enthusiastically supported by the community. He is one of the quintessential figures of all time to spark curiosity in himself and others. He interwove two of the best aspects of humanity: individual self-reliance while boldly advocating civic involvement to build community character. We should not make a mistake or take Franklin's achievement lightly just because he is historic. We can appreciate his accomplishment and how it opened doors for many less-educated Americans of that time.

Andrew Carnegie transformed the public library to its next level of innovation and potential by donating his money, time, and energy to establishing a free public library in more than 1,600 cities, towns, and villages across North America. Do we automatically think unfavorably on Carnegie because he revolutionized the steel industry and became wealthy? Or, like with Steve Jobs, who revolutionized the personal-technology industry, can we recognize and appreciate the genius of these two earlier individuals?

Carnegie wanted to make wealth a beneficial aspect of life that anybody could obtain, no matter what gender or race. A hundred years later, we may be tempted to pooh-pooh his *Gospel of Wealth*, a philosophical and practical how-to essay about the responsibility of philanthropy for those with excess income—but only if we haven't read it. His writings reveal a caring, intelligent observer of society at that time. Can we celebrate his brilliant idea to give the majority of his money to communities to build libraries? Carnegie, who learned the importance of celebrating his successes as a working boy in Pittsburgh, revamped the American public library. This transformation opened up opportunities for women and people of color to reading, learning, and changing their circumstances unlike ever before in history.

## Celebrate Your Community

More than six hundred guests pack the Miller Branch of the Howard County (MD) Library System each year to celebrate "Evening in the Stacks," a black-tie gala whose proceeds benefit A+ Partners in Education signature initiatives. A group of individuals in their 20s and 30s formed the Raven Society to hold rooftop "biergarten" parties, exhibit international artists celebrating text and word in art, and host author receptions in honor of the Free Library of Philadelphia. Similarly, a diverse group of cosmopolitans, the Pratt Contemporaries, holds a "Black and White Party" and other festive events to raise awareness of the Enoch Pratt Free Library in Baltimore.

"I didn't even know the Library had a rooftop," writes Anna Idler. At the event, she enjoyed wine and tasted local beers, and got to mingle with other young professionals in Philadelphia passionate about literature and the library. She posts on her blog, "There were ancient books to pose with to make us look studious—even more nerdy than we already are. To further this point we also wore glasses. The English major in me was in heaven. We had so much fun chatting with attendees and current members of the Raven Society . . . I love on their webpage that it lists one of their goals as building and maintaining an engaged community of lifelong learners."[1]

Although many of these literary-inspired celebrations are fundraisers, try throwing a party or bash or hullaballoo for the heck of it—simply to celebrate the library and your community! A party can help people lighten up and unlock the spirit of cooperation.

What are the strengths of your community? By recognizing and celebrating the good aspects of the world around us, librarians can use these strengths to help solve problems, grapple with challenges, and produce meaningful results. Librarians

Main Branch, Carnegie Library of Pittsburgh.

Howard County (MD) Library System's annual fundraising gala, Evening in the Stacks, features a different theme and attracts six hundred guests every year.

*Courtesy of Howard County Library System.*

The green roof on top the Free Library of Philadelphia Main Branch—a perfect spot for "biergarten" parties.

*Courtesy of Free Library of Philadelphia.*

can best serve our communities by riding the waves of curiosity and celebration to help communities thrive.

Pikes Peak Library District in Colorado Springs recognized the need to offer more technology, hands-on activities, and various small and large group meet-up spaces to better serve their constituents. A new library called Library 21c opened in summer 2015. Besides a large area of computers—known as Creative Computer Commons (C3)—Library 21c offers a makerspace with an array of opportunities to be creative, using high and low technologies such as 3-D printers, video recording and editing software, and sewing machines. A business-and-entrepreneurial center adds a special resource for new and seasoned entrepreneurs.

Lincoln County Public Libraries in Montana team up with their youngest writers and artists by asking for a piece of art or a short story that illustrates an idea, such as: A man sprints down the sidewalk, looking over his shoulder. Half a block away, someone is chasing and gaining on him. Why is the man running? Is he a good guy running from evil? Or is he the villain?

The University of Alberta Libraries have partnered with Edmonton Public Library to bring convenient public library services to members of the University of Alberta community: students can sign up for the L-Pass (library pass).

From a book review written by a teen at the Springfield–Greene County Library District in Missouri: "Part of me is infuriated with J. K. Rowling for killing that character but it made me realize that she is an amazing writer to have made me feel this way towards this certain character. She made some words off a page become a living, breathing soul who had a personality and a name . . . That is talent. I definitely recommend this book, *Harry Potter and the Half Blood Prince*, to any age group."

Lincoln Center for the Performing Arts brings free world-class concerts into local neighborhoods via the Queens Library. These concerts encompass a wide range of eclectic musical styles, traditions, and cultures. Joseph W. Polisi, president of The Juilliard School and author of *The Artist as Citizen*, makes a strong point that "the self-absorbed artist" model of the past cannot be followed in today's world to fully promote the arts. Similarly, the new librarian defies old stereotypes by setting aside self-absorption, timidity, and unfriendliness. As these and other institutions across the country (such as Opera in the Ozarks in Eureka Springs, Arkansas) reach out to share the joy of the performing arts, libraries can be active in sharing the joy of wisdom in a community.

Nashville Public Library created an award-winning collaboration with its schools called Limitless Libraries. Student ID cards can be automatically used as a public library card where students order books to be delivered the next day. The library provides space for an afterschool initiative offering classes in bike repair, robotics, fashion design, and art. Library puppeteers train schoolteachers to incorporate puppets, storytelling, and reading into all aspects of coursework. These and other efforts are tied to increasing student test scores and academic achievement.

## Tips on Celebrating and Collaborating

How can you *identify your library's strengths*? What can you learn from others? Keep in mind that these are the strengths of the library, which isn't necessarily the same as individual skills. These strengths increase the ability of the community to overcome its problems. For example, a library's strengths to help overcome low school-readiness scores will include not only offering early literacy programs but also using patience, discernment, and forgiveness throughout the collaborative effort. "What can I do with my strengths to make things better," asks Kristen Bodvin, outreach programming specialist, Carroll County (MD) Public Library.

How can you *pay attention to your community*? "Find inspiration in learning what keeps your community up at night," says Mary Hastler, CEO, Harford County (MD) Public Library. Libraries can stay current with community interests, such as self-publishing, antique cars, 3-D printing, and local music. Brooke Newberry, early literacy librarian, La Crosse (WI) Public Library, adds, "Think of your community. Look for success, yet be willing to fail to become a stronger outreach librarian."

*Asking the right questions* is a key to success, especially questions that challenge assumptions you've made. One question to ask is, what more can I do to help my community? Another is, how can I *listen and respond to each person* coming into the library? The answers you discover to tough questions and the actions you eventually take may surprise you. This formula of questioning, reflecting, and acting may test you in the short term, but can create an uplifting experience in the long run.

"Working collaboratively produces richer thinking and perspective. Potential possibilities increase in number and people share in success and failure and learn together," says Vailey Oehlke, director, Multnomah (OR) County Library, Public Library Association President, 2015–16. It's important to *be open to new ideas*. Amy Koester, Youth & Family Program coordinator, Skokie Public Library, Illinois, suggests, "We want to help the community without preconceived notions. We don't assume that our partners or everyone within an agency are already on the same page. If we don't know how to contribute, we figure out what is possible together. From small snapshots shared in discussions with partners, the full picture unfolds."

Elizabeth Mills, doctoral student, University of Washington iSchool, and codirector of ProjectVIEWS2, puts it this way: "I am fascinated by inspiration and the innovation that comes from this inspiration. I think as a researcher and writer I'm always looking for something that inspires a new direction to go, a new voice to explore in my work. Searching for inspiration, though, never works as well for me as leaving my mind open to opportunities to be inspired." Jennifer Hopwood, training coordinator, Southern Maryland Regional Library Association, adds, "In libraries, we need to find the ideas that will hold value for our own communities and not just copying something that XYZ library has done."

Exploring new ideas requires the ability to *be flexible*. As Betsy Diamant-Cohen, executive director, Mother Goose on the Loose, describes, "Be very open to new ideas when you are working in collaboration with others. A flexible attitude creates great energy and encourages new and sometimes surprising ideas. As you work together with someone, that personal connection often leads to other projects. I've worked in museums, libraries, and universities—the personal connection has been instrumental in growing a community collaboration." Emily Weak, Adult & Virtual Services librarian, City of Mountain View (CA) Public Library, echoes this principle: "Flexibility, being open to new ideas, and a bit of humor help me do collaborative work, whether it is creating a ukulele club, maintaining the seed library project, or partnering with storytime buddy, Cen Campbell, to lead sing-alongs for adults."

An anecdote from *A Personal Odyssey* by economist Thomas Sowell poignantly reminds us of the value of flexibility:

> In the summer of 1959, I worked as a clerk-typist at the U.S. Public Health Service in Washington. The people I worked for were very nice and I grew to like them. One day, a man had a heart attack at around 5 PM, on the side-walk outside our building. He was taken inside to the nurse's room, where he was asked if he was a government employee. If he were, he would have been eligible to be taken to a medical facility there. Unfortunately, he was not, so a phone call was made to a local hospital to send an ambulance. By the time this ambulance made its way through miles of rush-hour traffic, the man was dead. He died waiting for a doctor, in a building full of doctors. Nothing so dramatized for me the nature of a bureaucracy and its emphasis on procedures, rather than results.[2]

As we work hard, we can often *tap the spirit of joyful achievement*, which in turn opens up new opportunities. How can we celebrate our potential and our community?

> Joy can perhaps be best defined as the delight in achievement and accomplishment . . . every day can bring fresh achievements [large or small] of great value; thus every day can bring new joy . . . it becomes a habitual mood with which we greet every moment.[3]
>
> **—ROBERT LEICHTMAN, MD, AND CARL JAPIKSE, *CELEBRATING LIFE***

Each library and each library branch has a different community to serve and situations to address. Suggestions made in this book can be a starting place, but your best chance for success lies in celebrating what works and what doesn't work in pursuing collaborations. These types of strategies—reducing bureaucracy, cultivating discernment, using self-control, distinguishing between good and bad plans—can help libraries avoid becoming breeding grounds for narrow or negative thinking, which will stifle their staff members' ability to spark curiosity and solve problems within their organization and community.

"It's important to keep a truly open mind. Embrace the whole community, not just the part you can approve of," says Rebecca Haas, Programming & Outreach Services manager, Anne Arundel County (MD) Library. Here's where effective planning can help. The role of the librarian is to draw everyone in by promoting an open mind. It may be popular to trumpet specific causes, but a more general approach of engaging every member of the community can reap long-term support.

Imagine if Benjamin Franklin were alive today. He would be an unabashed promoter of everything that is good in his community. That is the role of the new librarian—to celebrate everything that is good in your town, city, or county in order to work from a place of strength, skill, and joyful celebration to handle the inevitable challenges.

The new librarian—whether new or experienced, young or old, with or without a graduate degree—needs courage, tough new thinking skills, and a big-picture focus. In a scenario with Franklin as a librarian today, he might say to his colleagues, "Although we made a mistake in how we handled thus and such project, we have enough skills, tolerance, and humor to figure out how to become stronger as a team and serve individuals and families better. We will do our best and know that the community spirit of collaboration will support us."

Libraries have often been treated as a stepchild with local governments or county commissioners or mayors, for example, making funding decisions that gravely affect services. For the last 285 years—ever since Franklin formed his Library Company in Philadelphia—libraries helped develop the American landscape. Today most libraries benefit from the community through tax support. The library, in return, gives the community character and focus. It establishes the right and proper bonds between schools, colleges, businesses, churches, and others.

A community may *want* a cookie-cutter library—a library identical to every other library in the country—but let's give it what it *needs*: a library that responds to the individuals in that community. The library has the potential to encourage people to define themselves as a community, what it means to be part of the community, and to collaborate and cooperate with each other. The real charm and power of a library is how it can respond to its community—connecting people, organizations, and businesses to each other. As a library worker, you'll find out what it means to fully collaborate as you start to work more in your community to enrich its life. The rule of reciprocity in the American custom of barn-raising creates mutual experience and an ongoing opportunity to celebrate the individual and celebrate the community. Our goal: the library supports the community as the community supports the library. In the spirit of collaboration and celebrating our successes, let's focus on making the library into an institution worth supporting for another 285 years—or more.

> Courage is what it takes to stand up and speak; courage is also what it takes to sit down and listen.
>
> **—WINSTON CHURCHILL**

Questions to ponder on celebrating success:

1. Do I celebrate every time a customer or patron comes into the library or uses an online service?
2. Do I "shut down" when confronted with what I can learn from great leaders of the past, like Benjamin Franklin and Andrew Carnegie, especially those who fall under the category of "dead white men"? If yes, why?
3. Do I ask myself on a regular basis questions such as, what more can I do to help my community? How can I listen and respond to each person coming into the library to bring out their best skills?
4. What does it mean to me to be self-reliant or self-sufficient? How does that differ from being isolated? How does that differ from being self-absorbed?

### Notes

1. Anna Idler, "Rooftops, Ravens & Reading Glasses," June 2, 2015, *Anna Idler Writes* (blog), https://annaidlerwrites.wordpress.com/2015/06/02/rooftops-ravens -reading-glasses/.
2. Thomas Sowell, *A Personal Odyssey* (New York: Free Press, 2000), 125.
3. Robert Leichtman, MD., and Carl Japikse, *Celebrating Life* (Atlanta: Enthea Press, 1976), 33–35.

# AFTERWORD

**As librarians learn to collaborate, we will help our communities reach the** goal of self-reliance. When communities discover the means for right collaboration and effective planning, they create a world full of opportunities for families to become self-reliant and to thrive. Self-reliance means translating ideas into meaningful activity—work, family, self-improvement—to benefit the community. That means people using resources like the library. Self-reliance requires learning to teach oneself. It is not self-absorption, but a rallying of the best within.

In part, this book was inspired by Margaret Stoltz, Dorothy's mother, who grew up "dirt poor" in western Pennsylvania. One of fifteen children, whose father was a coal miner, Marge became a nurse, instructor, wife, and mother with "a heart of gold." Before she died, Marge said, "I spent as much time as I could at the one-room school near our farm. I learned from older students and helped teach the younger ones. We all learned together." She added, "By the time I was sixteen years old, I saw myself as a nurse, but knew I had a lot more to learn. I worked during World War II in factories and studied algebra, biology, and many other subjects on my own in order to get accepted into nursing school. I ended up graduating from St. Luke's Nursing School in Chicago. If the schoolteachers, librarians, and my parents had not collaborated—and perhaps without realizing they were doing so—I would not have been as motivated to become a nurse." Marge's story suggests to us that the library is filled with treasures that we need to share with people.

Each library can discover their own treasure, such as books in the stacks, storytimes with puppets and bubbles, discussion events, digital media mentoring—and community partners. "Acres of Diamonds," a lecture by Russell Conwell, founder of Temple University, Philadelphia, gives us a valuable tip: "look in your own backyard" to find a treasure trove of skills, resources, opportunities, and friends.[1] Traveling in the Middle East in 1869, Conwell heard a story from one of his guides about a wealthy man who sells his farm to go on a journey in search of diamonds. The man never finds a diamond mine and dies exhausted and destitute in a foreign land. The new owner of the man's farm discovers an acre of diamonds down near the stream and becomes exceptionally wealthy. The original farmer overlooked the rich treasure in his own backyard. Let us not go on a pointless journey to build riches. A library misses its potential in a community if it doesn't share the talents of its staff to spark curiosity and promote its resources that can support people to be their best. We have a solid, rich treasure in the library. Each library can figure out how to identify its treasure, how to activate it, and how to get the word out in the community—often through our collaborative activities.

When a library brings out its best collaborative spirit to pool resources in the community, the whole community benefits. The triumph of a library inspires people to cooperate and work together. Libraries, schools, and community partners can learn to work together creatively. It's as easy as a regular storytime family welcoming a new family to the library and showing that it's okay for a two-year-old to wander about in storytime. Turning an institution like the public library into a practical and active community service that sparks curiosity doesn't happen by accident. We need to listen and respond to each person to improve our relationship with a community and tap its potential.

### Note

1. Russell H. Conwell, and Robert Shackleton, *Acres of Diamonds: All Good Things Are Possible, Right Where You Are, and Now!* (Lexington, KY: Feather Tail Press, 2009), 6–8.

# APPENDIXES

## How the Appendixes Are Organized

**APPENDIX A** is a simple yet effective planning worksheet called Growing My Community Collaboration. It offers questions to help you think through how to start or improve a collaborative effort.

**APPENDIX B THROUGH D** feature results-based accountability planning tools. The Leadership in Action Program provided a number of resource materials that groups can use to improve how they collaborate, address barriers that often get in the way of effective collaboration, and move from talk to action, leading to results.

**APPENDIX E** is a planning example from Earlier Is Easier, an organization in Colorado. It is a model of how one broad collaboration organizes their work in the community.

**APPENDIX F** is a collection of everyday wisdom from people in and outside the field of librarianship.

**APPENDIX G** refers to ALA Editions Web Extras, available for free at alastore.org.

**APPENDIX H** offers suggested reading.

# APPENDIX A

## Growing My Community Collaboration Worksheet

My collaboration idea is:

_____

_____

_____

_____

What partnerships already exist that can support this idea?

_____

_____

_____

_____

The needs of the audience are:

_____

_____

_____

_____

How will the collaboration meet the needs of the audience being served?
(Describe the benefits.)

_____

_____

_____

_____

_____

_____


I'll contact the following partners to explore this idea:

1. _____

2. _____

3. _____


Who else should be at the table? What will their roles/responsibilities be?

_____

_____

_____

_____

_____

_____


What services are already in place? What will need to be created?

_____

_____

_____

_____

_____

_____

What are the steps/activities needed to get the collaboration established and services delivered? (Create a time line to keep you on track.)

_____

_____

_____

_____

_____

_____

What will I need to spend money on? What sources of funding can be explored?

_____

_____

_____

_____

_____

_____

What will success look like? How will the collaboration measure success?
What tools/expertise will I need to measure success?

_____

_____

_____

_____

_____

_____

_____

*Adapted from Maryland's Division of Library Development & Services
and Carroll County (MD) Public Library.*

## Using Critical Incidents to Build Leadership Competence
Building on the work of CFAR (www.cfar.com)

**Leaders are tasked with solving problems that often represent persistent** and unyielding challenges. A critical incident is an event where you as a leader attempted to address a challenge and things did not turn out as planned. Analyzing these moments can yield significant insights and learning about you personally, about how you understand or carry out your role, and/or about how the system (the visible and invisible rules, relationships and dynamics of an organization) influences your leadership choices and opportunities.

The primary goal of critical incident analysis is to fully understand what happened and explore multiple ideas about why it happened the way it did. Critical incident analysis helps leaders to see things in a new way and to try something new.

### CRITICAL INCIDENT ANALYSIS: A THREE-STEP PROCESS
The learning from a critical incident is uncovered when you as a leader take these three steps to better understand what did not go well:

1. *Describe* the facts of the incident: what was intended, what actually happened, and who were the people involved.
2. *Diagnose* what led to the incident: what are *multiple* hypotheses about "why" it did not turn out well.
3. *Decide* what to do: what are new insights and possible next steps for trying something new.

## Getting Started

Think of an incident where things did not go well for you in your leadership role and where the issue or challenge is still present for you. Use an incident that is current and where—even now, with the benefit of hindsight—you're not exactly sure what you could have done to contribute to a better outcome. Jot some notes to yourself about who was involved, what was at issue, what you intended, and what happened. The incident should be one in which you had a conversation with the other person or people and where you will be talking or working with them again in the future.

### Step One: Describe What Happened

Identify a colleague who will listen and ask effective questions.

During this initial step, you describe to your colleague what happened. The description includes what you did, what you hoped would happen, and what did happen. Address these questions in your description:

What are the facts of what happened?

> **Example Fact:** "My colleague and I disagreed, and then the colleague talked to my boss."
>
> (*Tip: Focus on facts, not interpretations. For example: "My colleague undermined me."*)

After the initial description of the critical incident, your colleague asks fact-based clarifying questions. These questions illuminate what happened and create a deeper understanding of power dynamics, formal and informal roles, intentions of others, etc.

### Step Two: Diagnose—Generating Multiple Hypotheses

During this step, your colleague helps you to unpack the critical incident by generating and sharing more than one hypothesis as to what is really going on. In sharing hypotheses, the colleague refrains from problem solving, and you take the opportunity to listen with an open mind to gain new insights.

The following are areas to explore in generating hypotheses[*]:

» Person–role–system analysis to illuminate the leader's contribution to the incident
» Presence of adaptive and technical challenges and issues of loss
» Influence of race, class, culture
» Factors of trust, power, authority, and accountability
» Competing interests
» Types of conflicts (values, relationships, data, structural, language)

---

[*]These tools and frames as well as others can be found on RBLApps.com.

### *Step Three: Deciding—Next Steps Based on New Insights*

Based on what you have heard, you then reflect on the hypotheses and share your insights, especially those about your contribution to the incident. Using these new insights about the critical incident and about yourself and others, you then decide what you will do differently going forward and what steps you will take to address the situation in a new way.

## Trying It Yourself

### *Journal*

What is a situation that you are facing where you don't know how to move forward—a situation where you have attempted to address without success or with limited success?

- » What was the issue? Who was involved? What happened?
- » What did you intend?
- » What was your contribution to the incident?
- » Who will you invite to be your colleague analyzing your critical incident?
- » How will you share the critical incident analysis approach with them?

### Race to the Top–Early Learning Challenge
Leadership Academy for Early Childhood Advisory Councils
Results-Based Leadership Institute #1–Results-Based Accountability

## STRATEGIES INVENTORY

Begin an inventory of strategies implemented or planned in your jurisdiction. To simplify this task, please use the inventory template below.

| Strategy (label, brief description, with types of programs being implemented as part of the strategy) | Target Population (who, how many) | Partners (implemented by whom, where) | Data (if available) | Supports Which State Strategy/ Goal/Priority |
|---|---|---|---|---|
|  |  |  |  |  |
|  |  |  |  |  |
|  |  |  |  |  |
|  |  |  |  |  |
|  |  |  |  |  |
|  |  |  |  |  |

## Aligned Action Commitments for Early Childhood Advisory Councils
Action Plan Sample, November 16, 2012

| Name | Action(s) | With Whom | When | Contribution to the Result | Progress Made (to be reported at next session) |
|------|-----------|-----------|------|----------------------------|-----------------------------------------------|
| Dorothy | Meet leadership team of 5 | Sue, Joyce, Dorothy, Mary, Liza | Week of 11/26 | Compare notes of Results Based Accountability, start planning, confirm grant proposal | |
| | Assist with filling in membership gaps and writing of grant by team | Sue, Joyce, Dorothy, Mary, Liza | Dec | Fulfill requirements for early learning grant; expand membership | |
| | Help plan retreat(s) | Sue, Joyce, Dorothy, Mary, Liza | Dec/Jan | Get full Early Childhood Consortium on board | |

## Colorado Example
### Earlier Is Easier

**An excellent example of a successful–and large–collaborative project focused** on early childhood can be found in Colorado. The group, known as Earlier Is Easier, has created a website tailored to the needs of their parents and partners. The collaborative leadership created three documents for community partners: Partnership Background Information, Opportunities, and an Application to formally join the collaboration.

Here is a summary of the collaboration and those documents.

> Earlier Is Easier is a collaborative led by early childhood literacy professionals from the Denver Public Library, Reach Out and Read Colorado, and the Colorado Parent & Child Foundation. They have joined forces with more than 20 early childhood organizations to promote the value of interacting with children at these young ages. The collaborative created and maintains the EarlierIsEasier .org website.

## BACKGROUND INFORMATION
### A Collaborative Project of:

DENVER PUBLIC LIBRARY

where great stories begin™

COLORADO PARENT & CHILD FOUNDATION

## Mission

Earlier Is Easier promotes the value of interacting with children ages birth to three through song, play, talking, writing and reading to enhance development and help shape children's lives when brain development is most critical.

## Vision

Earlier Is Easier's vision is to have everyone understand the positive impact that early learning has not only on the child, but on society as a whole.

## What

> » Promote awareness through a messaging campaign (sharing mission and vision).
> » Leverage literacy partners in sharing message and their supporting work/services.
> » Focus specifically on the birth to three population in Denver.

## BACKGROUND AND RATIONALE

For more than 20 years, a growing body of research has provided compelling evidence that early learning is critical to the future success of children as they progress through school and through life. Children who have not learned essential pre-literacy skills prior to entering kindergarten are at an educational disadvantage, and they may never catch up with their pre-literate classmates. In 2008 the Denver Public Library created a long-range strategic plan with goals that focused on the importance of early learning for Denver children. This plan identified elements that would be most impactful in terms of successful outcomes for children. Research showed that from a child's birth through three years of age, effective communication between parents (and other primary care-givers) and their child is crucial to educational development of the child. Because of their busy schedules, it is difficult to reach these key individuals with messages about how to help their children develop pre-literacy skills. During the following three years, as the Library's plan for an early learning awareness campaign gradually emerged, it became clear that other organizations serving the needs of very young children were also trying to reach parents and caregivers with this vital information. But no one orga-nization had the resources required to accomplish the task. It would take a broad-based partnership to achieve the goal.

## HISTORY AND ACCOMPLISHMENTS-TO-DATE
### October 2010

Representatives from Denver Public Library, Reach Out and Read Colorado, Colorado Bright Beginnings, the Denver Mayor's Office for Education and Children, Denver Great Kids Head Start, Clayton Early Learning, and Mile High United Way met to explore the possibility of a cooperative venture to address early learning.

## April 2011–April 2012

Regularly scheduled meetings were held with representatives from Denver Public Library, Reach Out and Read Colorado and Colorado Bright Beginnings.

### Key Accomplishments during This Period

- » Crafting of mission and vision statement, as well as a logic model identifying inputs, activities, outputs, short-term outcomes, intermediate outcomes, and impact.
- » Crafting of an initial scope of work for a contract campaign manager.
- » Confirmation of audience targets: primary audience—parents and caregivers; secondary audience—concerned members of the community.

## May–August 2012

Denver Public Library, Reach Out and Read Colorado, and Colorado Parent & Child Foundation became official Founding Partners of the Earlier Is Easier Collaborative. The three Founding Partners represent three key locations for outreach to parents of children birth to three: public libraries (Denver Public Library), health settings (Reach Out and Read Colorado), and home settings (Colorado Parent & Child Foundation).

### Key Accomplishments during This Period

- » Establishment of roles and responsibilities for each of the Founding Partner organizations, culminating in a formal Partnership Agreement between the executive officers and boards of the three organizations.
- » Formal submission of proposal for seed money from the Piton Foundation.
- » Met with Lindsay Dolce to provide background on Earlier Is Easier and discuss alignment of this birth-to-three Denver-focused awareness campaign with the Colorado Reads birth-to-eight statewide campaign.
- » Interviews held with potential contract campaign managers. Selection of and contracting with the team of James Mejia and Andrew Hudson (Mejia/Hudson) as the contract campaign managers.

## August–September 2012

The Founding Partners continued to meet regularly to oversee the initial development of the campaign. University of Colorado graduate student Andrew Weiss began providing administrative support to Earlier Is Easier.

### Key Accomplishments during This Period

- » Mejia/Hudson created a six-month timeline outlining the development of the awareness plan.
- » Mejia/Hudson engaged in initial fact finding, interviewing 25 key leaders in the early literacy arena.

» Half-day retreat held to share interview responses across major areas such as: effective communication messages, monitoring and measuring literacy for children birth to three, influencing parents, other public information campaigns, potential resource competitors, and overall campaign success.

## October–December 2012

The Founding Partners and Mejia/Hudson continued to meet to outline initial steps toward the formal launch of the multimedia awareness campaign and to discuss engaging additional partners.

### Key Accomplishments during This Period

» Mejia/Hudson secured the creative services of Steve Miller, IdeaSource, who presented branding and logo design elements for Earlier Is Easier. The Earlier Is Easier logo and tagline: "Make the most of your child's first three years" were approved, with key messages of *read, sing, talk, play, write, laugh.*

» Mejia/Hudson and Miller developed the outline for the EarlierIsEasier.org website.

» Mejia/Hudson developed a draft budget for the multimedia awareness campaign, including projected costs for campaign administration; production costs; web development and maintenance; and advertising through print, transit, television, radio, Internet, e-mail, direct mail, events, and social media.

» The Founding Partners and Mejia/Hudson continued to strategize concerning partnerships. Organizational partners will include Endorsing Partners, Advisory Partners, and Supporting Partners.

## PARTNERSHIP OPPORTUNITIES

Earlier Is Easier was founded by early childhood literacy professionals from three organizations: the Denver Public Library, Reach Out and Read Colorado, and the Colorado Parent & Child Foundation. Scientific research in early childhood brain development has concluded that early literacy is a cornerstone of early learning. While parents want the best for their children, the research that shows the inherent value of interacting with children ages birth to three is not widely known. Bringing together like-minded professionals in early childhood education, a collaborative was created to promote awareness to the Denver community about the importance of birth-to-three early learning efforts.

Earlier Is Easier is seeking organizational partners to help shape, implement, and carry forward a multimedia awareness campaign that highlights the importance of interacting with children ages birth to three through singing, playing, talking, reading, writing, and laughing.

## Endorsing Partners
### Benefits
» Organization receives recognition as an Earlier Is Easier Endorsing Partner (including an organizational listing on EarlierIsEasier.org, as well as on collateral material as appropriate).

### Commitment
» Incorporate Earlier Is Easier messaging into your organizational work and include link to EarlierIsEasier.org on your organizational website.

## Advisory Partners
### Benefits
» Organization receives recognition as an Earlier Is Easier Advisory Partner (including an organizational listing on EarlierIsEasier.org, as well as on collateral material as appropriate).
» Credited cross-promotional content on the website and social media.
» Organization will be instrumental in helping to shape the birth to three awareness campaign, providing focused input and direction to the plan and its implementation.

### Commitment
» Incorporate Earlier Is Easier messaging into your organizational work and include link to EarlierIsEasier.org on your organizational website.
» Help identify and secure additional Supporting Partners and utilize organizational connections for the advancement of Earlier Is Easier.
» Actively participate in Earlier Is Easier planning meetings (held approx. quarterly) to advise the plan and help carry out its implementation.
» Provide birth-to-three early literacy content to EarlierIsEasier.org.

## Supporting Partners
### Benefits
» Organization receives additional marketing and promotional benefits as an Earlier Is Easier Supporting Partner (including a logo on EarlierIsEasier.org, advertising, and collateral as appropriate).
» Organization is welcome to participate in shaping the birth-three awareness campaign (see role for Advisory Partners above).

### Commitment
» Financial resources in the form of cash support, pro-bono or sponsored media support, pro-bono or sponsored collateral support, pro-bono or sponsored web maintenance.

» Supporting Partners may choose to participate in the activities outlined for Endorsing and Advisory Partners, but are not required to do so.

Contact Earlier Is Easier to customize your Supporting Partner program.

## PARTNERSHIP APPLICATION

Earlier Is Easier was founded by early childhood literacy professionals from three organizations: the Denver Public Library, Reach Out and Read Colorado, and the Colorado Parent & Child Foundation. Scientific research in early childhood brain development has concluded that early literacy is a cornerstone of early learning. While parents want the best for their children, the research that shows the inherent value of interacting with children ages birth to three is not widely known. Bringing together like-minded professionals in early childhood education, a collaborative was created to promote awareness to the Denver community about the importance of birth to three early learning efforts.

Earlier Is Easier is seeking organizational partners to help shape, implement, and carry forward a multimedia awareness campaign that highlights the importance of interacting with children ages birth to three through singing, playing, talking, reading, writing and laughing.

### Application Instructions

» Submit completed application to EarlierIsEasier@gmail.com by February 28, 2013.
» Applications should be signed by three individuals, including the individual who will represent the organization for Earlier Is Easier efforts, the Executive Director/President/CEO, and a signature from the leadership of the organization's Board of Directors.
» Applications will be reviewed by the Founding Partners and applicants will be notified by March 31, 2013.

### Application Type

(See Appendix for a description of the Partnership Types, Benefits, and Commitment.)

❑ Endorsing Partner
❑ Advisory Partner
❑ I am interested in becoming a Supporting Partner and would like Earlier Is Easier to contact me.

## General Information

NAME OF ORGANIZATION:

Organization Type:

- ❏ Governmental Entity
- ❏ Nonprofit Organization
- ❏ Grant-Making Foundation
- ❏ Corporation
- ❏ Media Outlet
- ❏ Other:

Organization's Website Address:

Earlier Is Easier Contact for Organization:

Contact E-mail:

Contact Telephone Number:

## Organizational Information

MISSION STATEMENT:

ORGANIZATION'S CURRENT PRIORITIES RELATED TO BIRTH-TO-THREE EARLY LITERACY IN DENVER:

WHY WE WANT TO BE PART OF EARLIER IS EASIER:

**For Advisory Partner Applications Only**

IDEAS TO EXPAND THE CURRENT PLAN/THINGS EARLIER IS EASIER SHOULD CONSIDER:

**For Advisory Partner and Supporting Partner Applications Only**

WHAT WE WANT TO BRING TO THE TABLE:

## Organizational Approvals

By signing this application, the organization hereby certifies that:

1. It has read and is committed to the mission and vision of *Earlier Is Easier*.
2. It has read and agrees with the expectations outlined for the type of partnership the agency has applied for.

| | |
|---|---|
| ***EARLIER IS EASIER*** <br> **CONTACT FOR ORGANIZATION** <br> (This is the individual that will participate in Earlier Is Easier activity on behalf of the organization.) | Print Name: <br><br> Title: <br><br> Signature: |
| **EXECUTIVE DIRECTOR APPROVAL** <br> (required) | Print Name: <br><br> Title: <br><br> Signature: |
| **BOARD OF DIRECTOR APPROVAL** <br> (required) | Print Name: <br><br> Title: <br><br> Signature: |

## Pondering Everyday Wisdom

**Librarians share wisdom wherever we find it. The greatest collaboration made** by library professionals is the collection of wisdom. As examples of nuggets of wisdom, we have included some in this appendix that helped in the writing of this book.

The best teacher is often our own experience. Learning and being inspired by others can be helpful, especially to develop our own thinking. Asking ourselves questions often elicits an inner wisdom to solve a problem or develop an idea. How do we respond when something doesn't go a certain way in a partnership? Do we hold on to wanting things to be "just so" even when they are not, or can we move past frustration in order to contribute more fully? If we make a mistake, do we dwell on it, or do we correct it and learn from it to do better next time? Can we see the humor in a situation, lighten up, and move on? These types of questions nudge us to think things through and become more effective.

This appendix draws on the everyday wisdom of people in and outside the field of librarianship, with or without a library degree, and from some of the world's great thinkers, leaders, and philosophers.

The way a team plays as a whole determines its success. You may have the greatest bunch of individual stars in the world, but if they don't play together, the club won't be worth a dime.

—**Babe Ruth**

One day, Gutenberg, perhaps after he'd drunk a goblet of wine, asked himself, "What if I took a bunch of these coin punches and put them under the force of the wine press so that they left their image on paper?" The resulting combination was the printing press and movable type.[1]

—Roger von Oech, author of
*A Whack on the Side of the Head: How You Can Be More Creative*

In his autobiography, Benjamin Franklin describes his plan of self-examination as a young man and his attempt to come to terms with twelve virtues, such as order, moderation, industry, and tranquility. He worked on these attributes all his life and mastered many of them. He added a thirteenth virtue after a friend "kindly informed" Franklin that he had a tendency to be overbearing. Franklin added humility to his list with the notation "Imitate Jesus and Socrates." He reports on his progress:

"I struggled with humility . . . you will see it, perhaps, often in this history; for even if I could conceive that I had completely overcome it, I should probably be proud of my humility."[2]

—BENJAMIN FRANKLIN

We may sometimes start a collaboration with one Head Start class and their families never knowing where it will lead. Other times we may start with someone high up in administration, even at a state or national level. The key point to remember is that we need to interpret and connect our goals, resources, activities, and services into language that of each partner so that they can better understand what we can offer. In so doing, we also are better able to understand our partners' goals and services. The process can take time and perseverance and comes with great rewards for all.

—Saroj Ghoting, author and early childhood literacy consultant

Nearly all men can stand adversity, but if you want to test a man's character, give him power.

—Abraham Lincoln

The urge to save humanity is almost always a false front for the urge to rule.

—H. L. Mencken, Baltimore journalist and author

When Helen Keller was living in New York during her college days at Radcliffe, she met Mark Twain. She "read" from his lips as he told her stories. Helen's description of that meeting in her autobiography tells us something compelling about bringing out the best in each other:

He has his own way of thinking, saying and doing everything. I feel the twinkle of his eye in his handshake. Even while he utters his cynical wisdom in an indescribably droll voice, he makes you feel that his heart is a tender Iliad of human sympathy.[3]

—HELEN KELLER

The library is a valuable, never-ending source of materials and knowledge which I use regularly to teach my kids about what is important in life.

—Valerie Coles, mother in Atlanta, Georgia

In his essay on self-reliance, Ralph Waldo Emerson, writes about the power within each person to depend on and trust ourselves. We may look outward to favorable events to raise our spirits to no avail, it is a temporary experience.

Nothing can bring you peace but yourself. Nothing can bring you peace but the triumph of principles.[4]

—RALPH WALDO EMERSON

The center of a great tornado is a point of peace. And thus it is with all the storms of life. They lead to peace if you are not a leaf.

—Alice Bailey

I attribute my success to this: I never gave or took any excuse.

—Florence Nightingale

The mind is everything. What you think, you become.

—Buddha

What better way to help a community thrive than for libraries and schools to cooperate, collaborate, and succeed together?

—Andrew Medlar, 2015/16 President, Association for Library Service to Children

I never considered a difference of opinion in politics, in religion, in philosophy, as cause for withdrawing from a friend.

—Thomas Jefferson

The reality is that most people are not striving to be a "great person in history" . . . But we all still strive to have our lives matter, to close our eyes for the final time knowing that even a small piece of the world is better for our having been here.[5]

—Paul G. Stoltz and Erik Weihenmayer, *The Adversity Advantage*

It is our pleasure to help the community in any way we can.

—Christy Estrovitz, youth services manager, San Francisco Public Library

No man will make a great leader who wants to do it all himself, or to get all the credit for doing it.

—ANDREW CARNEGIE

It is probably a mistake to assume that whatever little children touch they will destroy . . . it is only by handling and using objects that children can learn the right way to handle them . . . [Maria] Montessori showed that very little children could easily be taught to move, not just exuberantly, but also deftly, precisely, and gently.[6]

—John Holt, *How Children Learn*

A library is all about asking what we can do for you—the parent, the business owner, the person interested in local history, the county commissioner.

—Tony Eckard, director of finance, Carroll County (MD) Public Library

To live is so startling it leaves little time for anything else.

—Emily Dickinson, poet

## Notes

1. Roger von Oech, *A Whack on the Side of the Head: How You Can Be More Creative* (New York: Warner Books, 1998), 8.
2. Benjamin Franklin, *The Autobiography & Other Writings* (New York: Bantam Classic, 1982), 85.
3. Helen Keller, *The Story of My Life* (New York: Bantam Classic, 2005), 100–01.
4. Ralph Waldo Emerson, *Essays* (Reading, PA: Spencer, 1936), 59.
5. Paul G. Stoltz and Erik Weihenmayer, *The Adversity Advantage* (New York: Fireside Books, 2006), 251.
6. John Holt, *How Children Learn*, rev. ed. (Reading, MA: Perseus Books, 1983), 33.

# APPENDIX G

## Collaboration in Practice

*Available free at www.alaeditions.org/webextras.*

WEB EXTRA A

### CIRCLE OF CONFLICT ADAPTATION

Using six sources of conflict—values, relationships, data, interests, language, and structure—this two-page resource gives tips on how to take action and resolve conflicts.

WEB EXTRA B

### ARE YOU IN HIGH ACTION & HIGH ALIGNMENT?

Victoria Goddard-Truitt and Jolie Pillsbury present a few easy-to-use tools in this two-page article on how to assess one's commitment level and use data effectively in order to get better results.

WEB EXTRA C

### ACCOUNTABILITY RESEARCH BRIEF

The Results Based Leadership Collaborative at the University of Maryland School of Public Policy offers key findings from several studies that suggest strategies to hold yourself and others accountable.

WEB EXTRA D

### MBTI FOUR CONFLICT PAIRS

Summarized tips for getting along and working more effectively from a Leadership in Action Program training using Myers-Briggs Type Indicators.

# APPENDIX H

## Suggested Reading

Boog, Jason. *Born Reading: Bringing Up Bookworms in a Digital Age—From Picture Books to eBooks and Everything in Between*. New York: Touchtone, 2014.

Calcaterra, Regina. *Etched in Sand: A True Story of Five Siblings Who Survived an Unspeakable Childhood on Long Island*. New York: HarperCollins, 2013.

Campbell, Cen, Claudia Haines, Amy Koester, and Dorothy Stoltz. *Media Mentorship in Libraries Serving Youth*. Position paper written for the Association for Library Services to Children, 2015.

Carnegie, Andrew. *The Autobiography of Andrew Carnegie*. New York: Houghton Mifflin, 1920.

———. *The Gospel of Wealth*. 1901; Marble Hill, GA: Kudzu House, 2008.

De Bono, Edward. *Creativity Workout: 62 Exercises to Unlock Your Most Creative Ideas*. Berkeley, CA: Ulysses Press, 2008.

———. *Lateral Thinking: Creativity Step by Step*. NY: Harper Perennial, 1970.

———. *Six Thinking Hats*. Revised edition. New York: Bay Back Books, 1999.

Diamant-Cohen, Betsy, ed. *Children's Services: Partnerships for Success*. Chicago: ALA Editions, 2010.

Donohue, Chip, ed. *Technology and Digital Media in the Early Years: Tools for Teaching and Learning*. New York: Routledge, 2014.

Earlier Is Easier. www.earlieriseasier.org.

Emerson, Ralph Waldo. *Essays*. Reading, PA: Spencer Press, 1936. (Or any copy of Emerson's *Essays*.)

Franklin, Benjamin. *The Autobiography of Benjamin Franklin & Other Writings*. New York: Bantam Books, 1982. (Or any copy of Franklin's autobiography.)

Friedman, Mark. *Trying Hard Is Not Good Enough: How to Produce Measurable Improvements for Customers and Communities*. Booksurge, 2009.

Frydman, Bert, Iva Wilson, and JoAnne Wyer. *The Power of Collaborative Leadership: Lessons for the Learning Organization*. Boston: Butterworth Heinemann, 2000.

Gallinsky, Ellen. *The Mind in the Making: The Seven Essential Life Skills Every Child Needs*. New York: William Morrow, 2010.

Guernsey, Lisa. *Screentime: How Electronic Media—From Baby Videos to Educational Software—Affects Your Young Child*. New York: Basic Books, 2007.

Guernsey, Lisa, and Levine, Michael H. *Tap, Click, Read: Growing Readers in a World of Screens*. San Francisco: Jossey-Bass, 2015.

Holt, John. *How Children Learn*. Reading, MA: Perseus Books, 1964.

Japikse, Carl. *The Enlightened Management Journal*. Alpharetta, GA: Ariel Press, 1995.

Keller, Helen. *Optimism*. Atlanta: Enthea Press. First published in 1901. This edition issued in 2006.

——— . *The Story of My Life*. New York: Bantam Dell, 2005.

Koester, Amy, ed. *Young Children, New Media, and Libraries: A Guide for Incorporating New Media into Library Collections, Services, and Programs for Families and Children Ages 0-5*. 2015. https://littleelit.files.wordpress.com/2015/06/final-young-children-new-media-and-libraries-full-pdf.pdf.

Leichtman, Robert R., MD, and Carl Japikse. *Celebrating Life*. Atlanta: Enthea Press, 1976.

Maryland State Department of Education. *Supporting Every Young Learner: Maryland's Guide to Early Childhood Pedagogy Birth to Age 8*. January 2015. http://192.168.1.1:8181/www.marylandpublicschools.org/msde/divisions/child_care/docs/PedagogyGuide-LearningStandards_042015.pdf.

Neuman, Susan B., and Donna C. Celano. *Giving Our Children a Fighting Chance: Poverty, Literacy, and the Development of Information Capital*. New York: Teachers College Press, 2012.

Oakley, Ed, and Doug Krug. *Leadership Made Simple*. Dallas: Enlightened Leadership Solutions, 2007.

Palfrey, John. *BiblioTech: Why Libraries Matter More Than Ever in the Age of Google*. New York: Basic Books, 2015.

Ready at Five. www.readyatfive.org.

Smallwood, Carolyn, ed. *Librarians as Community Partners*. Chicago: ALA Editions, 2010.

Zero to Three. http://zerotothree.org.

# INDEX

## A

A+ Partners in Education, 66, 134
"Accountability Research Brief" (Results Based Leadership Collaborative at the University of Maryland School of Public Policy), 171
Achor, Shawn, 71
"Acres of Diamonds" (Conwell), 141–142
adversity, 114–117
*The Adversity Advantage* (Stoltz & Weihenmayer), 168
Aligned Action Commitments for Early Childhood Advisory Councils, Action Plan Sample, 155
ALSC (Association for Library Service to Children), 24, 108
*American Notes* (Dickens), 107
*Apology* (Plato), 10
appendixes
    Aligned Action Commitments for Early Childhood Advisory Councils, Action Plan Sample, 155
    Collaboration in Practice, 171
    Colorado Example, Earlier is Easier, 157–164
    Growing My Community Collaboration Worksheet, 145–147
    organization of, 143
    Pondering Everyday Wisdom, 165–168
    Race to the Top—Early Learning Challenge, 153
    Suggested Reading, 173–174
    Using Critical Incidents to Build Leadership Competence, 149–151
"Are You in High Action & High Alignment?" (Goddard-Truitt & Pillsbury), 171

Aristotle, 47
Articles of Confederation
    collaboration for creation of, 85
    debate about, 90–91
    replacement of, 81
*The Artist as Citizen* (Polisi), 136
Arup, Jens, 92
Association for Library Service to Children (ALSC), 24, 108
*The Atlantic*, 122

## B

Bailey, Alice, 167
Baltimore County (MD) Public Library, 9
"barn-raising," xv
"Battle of the Books" reading contests, 65–66
Beegan, Nini, 132–133
Beethoven, Ludwig van, 112, 113
"begin with the end in mind" habit, 49
Bell, Alexander Graham, 107
Bertot, John, 114
*Bits and Pieces Make a Boot* (song), 50
Bodvin, Kristen, 137
Bolt, Nancy, 126–127
Book Buggy, 126
Books & Bars, 56
Borge, Victor, 71
Boynton, Sandra, 6
brain, 5
brainstorming, 32, 33
Bridgman, Laura, 107
Browning, Elizabeth Barrett, 6–7

Buddha, 167
bureaucracy
    becoming less bureaucratic, 20–22
    description of, 17
    loss of trust/common vision with, 19–20
    reducing, 18–19
bureaucrats, 17
Burns, Robert, 82

**C**
Calcaterra, Regina, 99–100
Campana, Katie, 20
Campbell, Cen, x, 138
Carnegie, Andrew
    Enoch Pratt and, 117
    on funding libraries, 52
    on leadership, 168
    literacy goal of, 63
    model for philanthropic work pioneered by,
        48
    on starting with vision, 49
    success of, 133–134
Carnegie Library of Pittsburgh, 48, 135
Caroline County (MD) Library, 105
Carroll County (MD) Early Childhood
    Consortium, 114, 116–117
Carroll County (MD) Judy Center
    collaborative work of, ix–x
    kindergarten assessment of, 116
Carroll County (MD) Public Library
    Battle of the Books, 66
    collaborative work of, ix–x
    decorative pumpkin patch at, 18
    kindergarten assessment, 114, 116–117
    learning organization strategy, 114
    Squishy Circuit, 106
    timing for early childhood efforts, 71–72
Cecil County (MD) Public Library
    Cecil Station Early Learning Centers, 39
    SPARK bookmobile program, 88
Celano, Donna C., 105–106
Celebrating Life (Leichtman & Japikse), 4, 138
celebration
    benefits of, 131
    library celebration of collaboration, 4–6
    library leading the way to, 6–7
    to promote library services, 131–132
    questions on celebrating success, 140
    tapping spirit of, 132–134
    tips on celebrating/collaborating, 137–140
challenges, 82–85
Chan, Zoie, 67
Charlotte's Web (White), 9, 10

cheerfulness, 99–100
Chesnut, Mary Boykin, 38
children, Fred Roger's work with, 39–42
Chisholm, Dr., 107
chunking things down, 56–57, 59
Churchill, Clementine, 128
Churchill, Winston
    collaboration with Roosevelt, 121–122, 126
    on courage, 140
    as leader, 127–128
    relationship with Roosevelt, 129
Circle of Conflict Adaptation resource, 171
Clemens, Samuel (Mark Twain), 167
Coles, Valerie, 167
collaboration
    avoiding problems, 81–82
    barn-raising, xv
    bureaucracy and, 17–22
    celebrating/collaborating, tips on, 137–140
    core of strength/generosity, 122–125
    cowpokes story to illustrate, x–xi
    Earlier is Easier collaboration, 157–164
    Inspired Collaboration, organization of, xvi
    leaders, learning from great, 127–130
    leadership for, 126–127
    Leadership in Action Program, 125–126
    library celebration of, 4–6
    library leading the way to, 6–7
    library's role, questions about, 3–4
    meeting challenges, 82–85
    opportunities with, 141–142
    questions about, 130
    as shared mission, 10–12
    as symphony, 111–113
    tie between Britain and United States during
        World War II, 121–122
    tips for healthy community collaboration,
        12–13
Collaboration in Practice appendix, 171
Colorado, Earlier is Easier project, 157–164
Colorado Parent & Child Foundation, 157–164
Columbus (OH) Metropolitan Library
    Agape family at, 129
    Ready to Read Corps, 25–26, 127
communication
    bureaucracy and, 21, 22
    engagement, one person at a time, 98
    Fred Rogers on, 97
    for healthy community collaboration, 12
community
    celebrating/collaborating, tips on, 137–140
    celebration, tapping spirit of, 132–134
    celebration of, 134–137

desire to learn/grow, 23
   library celebration of, 131–132
   library collaboration with, benefits of, 141–142
   library meeting challenges to help, 82–85
   self-reliance goal, 141
community, engaging
   express cheerfulness/kindness, 99–100
   hire staff with compassion, 98–99
   learning tools, offering many, 100
   librarian's service, 97–98
   one person at a time, 98
   questions about, 102
   saying "Yes," 100–102
community collaboration
   core of strength/generosity, creation of, 122–125
   joy of, 5
   leaders, learning from great, 127–130
   leadership for, 126–127
   Leadership in Action Program, 125–126
   questions about, 130
   tie between Britain and United States during World War II, 121–122
   tips for healthy, 12–13
compassion, 98–99
Congress of the Confederation, 81–82
Conner, Marisa, 9
content, 104
context, 104
Conwell, Russell, 141–142
core of generosity, 122–125
core of strength, 122–125
corporate support, 33–36
Coteaching Reading Comprehension Strategies in Elementary School Libraries: Maximizing Your Impact (Moreillon), 82
Courie, Amanda, 105
Covey, Stephen
   on principles and goals, 49
   on priorities, 55
   on setbacks, 4
Craig (AK) Public Library, 100
critical incident analysis, 149–151
Crow, Sherry R., 87–89
curiosity
   community programming and, 98
   engagement, one person at a time, 98
   learn to think effectively, 91–95
   library support of development of, 89–91
   media mentoring for, 108
   questions about, 95–96
   saying "yes" to spark, 100–102

   study on students' curiosity, 87–89
   technology/learning, making fun and practical, 105, 106
Czarnecki, Elaine, 26–27

**D**
Dahms-Stinson, Nancee, 24–25
Dave Clark Five, 50
Davis, Denise, 113
de Bono, Edward, 91–93
Denton Independent School District, 125
Denton Public Library, 124–125
Denton Television, 125
Denver Public Library, 157–164
Diamant-Cohen, Betsy, 138
Dickens, Charles, 107
Dickinson, Emily, 168
DiCristofaro, Catherine, 94
discernment, 32–36
Dixon, Jess, 11–12
Donald, David Herbert, 74–75
Donohue, Chip, 105
Dothan Houston County (AL) Library System, 65
Dresang, Eliza, 21
Drucker, Peter, 32

**E**
Earlier is Easier project, 157–164
Early Learning and Children's Media, Fred Rogers Center, 40
Eastern Air Lines, 70, 74
Eckard, Tony, 168
ECRR
   See Every Child Ready to Read @ your library
Edmonton Public Library, 136
Edwards, Lindsay, 117
Emerson, Ralph Waldo
   on character, 121
   on instruction, 23
   on joy, 131
   on respecting the pupil, 22
   on self-reliance, 167
emotional development
   in early childhood, 37
   pretend-play activities for, 39
   self-control, acting with, 38–39
   what Fred Rogers would do, 39–42
engagement
   avoiding problems, 81–82
   challenges, meeting, 82–85
   express cheerfulness/kindness, 99–100
   hire staff with compassion, 98–99
   learning tools, offering many, 100

engagement (*continued*)
    librarian's service, 97–98
    one person at a time, 98
    questions about, 102
    saying "Yes," 100–102
enlighten humanity purpose
    collaboration for, 9–10
    discernment and, 33
    future of libraries and, 63
    library staff and, 21
    love of learning and, 38
    meeting challenges for, 83
    plan to fulfill, 70
    right things emerge from, 23
    tapping strength of whole for, 50
    as underlying purpose of library, 6
Enoch Pratt Free Library, Baltimore, MD
    "Black and White Party," 134
    creation of, 117–118
    Fairy Tale Extravaganza, 115
    green roof on top of, 135
    Leadership in Action Program collaboration,
        126
Estrovitz, Christy, 168
*Etched in Sand: A True Story of Five Siblings Who
    Survived an Unspeakable Childhood on Long Island*
    (Calcaterra), 99–100
Every Child Ready to Read @ your library (ECRR)
    Baltimore County's use of, 25
    for kindergarten assessment, 116
    toolkit offerings, 24
everyday greatness
    adversity, using to your advantage, 114–117
    collaboration as symphony, 111–113
    questions about, 118
    uplifting quality of human life, 117–118
excellence
    early literacy programs at libraries, 24–26
    Elaine and Gilda Roadshow, 26–27
    library's purpose to enlighten humanity, 23
    tapestry of, 28–29

**F**
family, 132
feedback, 76
Feldman, Sari, 83–84
Fernandes, Rick, 40–41
Ferrera, Vincent P., 39
*The Fifth Discipline: The Art and Practice of the
    Learning Organization* (Senge), 91
"First Card" service, 126
flexibility, 138
follow through
    fictional example of, 72–74

library director, importance of, 74–76
    questions about, 76
    timing for, 71–72
forgiveness, 128
Franklin, Benjamin
    on cooperation, 81–82
    creation of library, 55–56
    in France, 95
    on growth/progress, 81
    on humility, 166
    Junto group of, xvi
    literacy goal of, 63
    as modern librarian, 139
    priorities in creation of library, 56–57
    success of, 133
    use of humor, 90–91
    what he would do today, 57–59
fray, staying above
    core values, 37–38
    self-control, 38–39
    what Fred Rogers would do, 39–42
Fred Rogers Center Early Learning Environment, 69
Free Library of Philadelphia, 67–68
Fritchie, Barbara, 122
*From Values to Action: The Four Principles of Values-
    Based Leadership* (Kraemer), 37–38
funding, 48, 52
fundraisers, 134
future
    good plan embraces progress, 64–68
    good plan looks towards, 62–64

**G**
Gauthier, Alain, 56
generosity, core of, 122–125
Ghoting, Saroj, 166
Gibbs, Terri, 124
*Giving Our Children a Fighting Chance: Poverty,
    Literacy, and the Development of Information
    Capital* (Neuman & Celano), 105–106
goals
    need principles, 49–50
    prioritizing, 38
Goddard-Truitt, Victoria, 171
*Gospel of Wealth* (Carnegie), 134
Grafwallner, Rolf, x
Graham, Barbara, 24
Gray, Andrew, 67
Great Britain, 121–122, 126
Grinband, Jack, 39
Gross, Valerie, 66
group discussion, 32, 33
Growing My Community Collaboration
    Worksheet, 145–147

growth, 82–85
Guernsey, Lisa, 104, 106–107

**H**

Haines, Claudia, 26
Harford County (MD) Public Library, 123–124, 125
Harrod, Kerol, 124–125
Harvey-Jones, John, 50
Hass, Rebecca, 139
Hastler, Mary, 123–124, 137
Hayden, Carla, 117–118
Haywood, Carolyn, 68
Hesse, Hermann, 103
Hildebrandt, Irene, 66
Hobbes, Thomas, 91
*The Hobbit* (Tolkien), 31
Holt, John, 168
Homer (AK) Public Library, 27
Hopwood, Jennifer, 137
*How Children Learn* (Holt), 168
Howard County (MD) Library System
    Battle of the Books, 66
    "Evening in the Stacks" celebration, 134, 135
    hovercraft by HiTech students, 35
"Humans Optimize Decision Making by Delaying Decision Onset" (Teichert, Ferrera, & Grinband), 39
humor, 90

**I**

ideas, 137–138
Idler, Anna, 134
Illinois, Strengthening Families model, 98–99
Imercive, 76
implementation
    follow through, 71–74
    library director, importance of, 74–76
    of plan, 69–71
    questions about, 76
insight
    discernment, cultivation of, 32–36
    planning process, 31
Isaacson, Walter, 57

**J**

Japikse, Carl, 4, 138
Jefferson, Thomas
    on Articles of Confederation, 85
    on Benjamin Franklin, 95
    on Congress of the Confederation, 81–82
    on difference of opinion, 168
    on humor, 90–91

Johns Hopkins University, 26–27
Jones, Kendra, 133
joy, 113, 138
Junto group, xvi, 55–57

**K**

Kamin, Jeff, 56
Keller, Helen
    on Beethoven's *Ninth Symphony*, 112
    on good, 104
    on Mark Twain, 167
    on optimism, 103
    transformation of, 107–108
kindness, 99–100
Kirby, Lee, 49
Kluver, Carisa, 105
Knight, Angie, 66
Koester, Amy, 137
Kraemer, Harry, 37–38
Kuipers, Tara, xv

**L**

La Crosse (WI) Public Library, 83
LAP (Leadership in Action Program), 126
lateral thinking, 91
Latrobe (PA) Public Library, 41
leadership
    for community collaboration, 126–127
    discernment for, 32
    leading from any position, 94–95
    success of leaders, celebration of, 133–134
    Using Critical Incidents to Build Leadership Competence, 149–151
Leadership in Action Program (LAP), 126
"Leading from Any Position" training, 94–95
Lear, Edward, 122, 129
learning
    effective thinking, 91–95
    love of learning value, 38
    students' curiosity for, 87–89
    technology/learning, making fun and practical, 105–108
learning organization, 114
learning tools, 100
Ledermann, Molly, 97–98
Leichtman, Robert, 4, 138
Li, Junlei, 40
librarians
    adversity, using to your advantage, 114–117
    core of strength/generosity, creation of, 122–125
    discernment, cultivation of, 32–36
    effective thinking, 91–95
    engagement, one person at a time, 98–102

librarians (*continued*)
　hiring staff with compassion, 98–99
　leaders, learning from great, 127–130
　library service of, 97–98
　as media mentors, 106–107
　partnerships, skills for, 27–29
　value of collaboration, 7
library
　adversity, using to your advantage, 114–117
　bad/good plans, distinguishing between, 62–64
　Benjamin Franklin's creation of, 55–57
　bureaucracy in, 17–22
　celebrating/collaborating, tips on, 137–140
　celebration of collaboration, 4–6
　celebration of community, 134–137
　celebration to promote library services,
　　131–132
　collaboration, opportunities with, 141–142
　community, engaging, 97–102
　community collaboration, 121–130
　curiosity, support of development of, 89–91
　early literacy programs at, 24–26
　good plan embraces progress, 64–68
　leading collaboration/celebration, 6–7
　meeting challenges, 82–85
　number of/use of, 52
　planning, step-by-step process of, 47–49
　purpose of library in society, 50
　role in collaboration, questions about, 3–4
　service to community, 23
　shared mission with school, 10–12
　technology/learning, making fun and
　　practical, 105–108
　transformative power of, 103–104, 113
　value of collaboration, questions about, 7
library café program, 24, 84, 98–99
Library Company of Philadelphia, 55–57, 59
library director, 74–76
*Library Larry's Big Day* (television show),
　124–125
Limitless Libraries, 136
Lincoln, Abraham, 74–75, 166
Lincoln Center for the Performing Arts, 136
Lincoln County Public Libraries, Montana, 136
Lindsay, Nina, 84
literacy
　early literacy programs at libraries, 24–26
　Elaine and Gilda Roadshow, 26–27
　kindergarten assessment of, 114, 116–117
literature, reading great, 93–94
"Little Leapers" science kit collection, 124
LittleeLit.com, x
Littlefield, Jamie, 93–94

Livingston, Richard, 93–94
Love Is Not Enough Parent Cafés, 99

**M**
Mackey, Sarah, 127
magic
　questions about, 108–109
　technology/learning, making fun and
　　practical, 105–108
　of transformation, 103–104
Mannes, Marya, 37
Martinez, Gilda, 26–27
Maryland, early literacy public library model, 6
Maryland Model for School Readiness, 116
Masie, Elliott, 89
MBTI Four Conflict Pairs resource, 171
McComb, Sara, 41–42
media mentors, 106–107, 108
mediocrity, 27–29
Medlar, Andrew, 168
Mencken, H. L., 166
mentoring, 106–107
Mill, John Stuart, 17
Mills, Elizabeth, 137
Missoula (MT) Public Library, 97–98
*Mister Rogers' Neighborhood* (television show), 40–41
Mitchell, Susan
　collaborative work of, ix–x
　common mission story, 11–12
*Moo, Baa, La La La!* (Boynton), 6
Moreillon, Judi, 82

**N**
Nashville Public Library, 136
needs
　finding out what community needs, 123
　library for community, 139–140
Neuman, Susan B., 105–106
New York Public Library, 10
Newberry, Brooke, 137
Nightingale, Florence, 167
*Nonsense Rhymes* (Lear), 122, 129
*North American Review*, 52
Nowak, Keith, 76

**O**
"Ode to Joy" (Schiller), 113
Oehlke, Vailey, 137
"On Listening to Lectures" (Plutarch), 89
one person at a time, 98–102
Orange County Library System, Florida,
　Chickasaw Branch of, 23
orchestra metaphor, 111–113

**P**

Pandita, Sakya, 6
parents
  common mission with library, 11–12
  engagement with library, 84
  as first teachers, 63, 71, 75
  library collaboration with, 5, 6
  library follow-through work with, 73–74
  storytime for early literacy, 26–27
  technology mentoring and, 106–107
Parents as Teachers (PAT) curriculum, 116
partner, ix
partnership, ix–x
  *See also* collaboration
Pequot Library, Southport, Connecticut, 66–67
*A Personal Odyssey* (Sowell), 138
Peters, Kris, 84–85
Pierce County (WA) Library System, 51, 90
Pikes Peak Library District, Colorado Springs, 136
Pillsbury, Jolie, 171
planning
  avoiding problems, 81–82
  bad plan, examples of, 61–62
  bad/good plans, distinguishing between,
    62–64, 68
  celebration of success and, 139
  discernment, cultivation of, 32–36
  essential role of, 31
  for everyday greatness, 112
  follow through, 71–74
  good plan embraces progress, 64–68
  implementation of, library director and,
    74–76
  implementation of plan, 69–71
  lack of, 50–53
  meeting challenges for growth, 82–85
  plan in action, 47–48
  prioritizing work, 56–57
  questions about, 53
  starting with end in mind, 49–50
  as step-by-step process, 48–49
  what Benjamin Franklin would do, 57–59
Plato, 10, 104
playing, 24
Plutarch, 87, 89
point-of-passion experience, 88–89
Polisi, Joseph W., 136
pondering, 33
  *See also* questions
Pondering Everyday Wisdom appendix, 165–168
Pratt, Enoch, 117–118
Pratt Contemporaries, 134
principles, 49–50

prioritizing
  chunk it down, 56–57
  Stephen Covey on, 55
  what Benjamin Franklin would do, 57–59
Procter & Gamble (P&G), 63–64
progress, 64–68
ProjectVIEWS2, 20, 21
Public Library Association, 24

**Q**

quality of human life, 117–118
Queens Library, 136
questions
  on adversity/everyday greatness, 118
  asking right questions, as key to success, 137
  on community engagement, 102
  on good/bad plans, distinguishing between,
    68
  on meeting challenges, 85
  on planning, 53
  on sparking curiosity, 95–96
  on staying above the fray, 42
  on transformation/magic, 108–109

**R**

Race to the Top—Early Learning Challenge, 153
Racing to Read program, 24–25
railroads, 61–62
Raven Society, 134
Reach Out and Read Colorado, 157–164
reading
  "Battle of the Books" reading contests, 65–66
  early literacy programs at libraries, 24–26
Ready to Read Corps, 127, 129
reconstruction, 74–75
Reed, Caroline, 97–98
Reif, Kathleen, ix
relationships
  avoiding problems, 81–82
  library building relationships with
    community, 82–85
  *See also* collaboration
respect, 22
Results Based Leadership Collaborative at the
  University of Maryland School of Public Policy,
  171
Rice, Colin, 100
Rickenbacker, Eddie, 69, 70, 74
Ridgeway, Jeff, 66
Riordan, Ellen, 22, 126
Rogers, Fred
  on communication, 97
  on emotional independence, 69

Rogers, Fred (*continued*)
    on helpers, 42
    plan of, 76
    work with children, 39–42
Rogers, Will, 33
Roosevelt, Eleanor, 122
Roosevelt, Franklin Delano
    collaboration with Churchill, 121–122, 126
    as leader, 127, 128
    relationship with Churchill, 129
Rowling, J. K., 136
Ruth, Babe, 165

**S**

San Francisco Public Library
    Early Literacy Buffet, closing, 11
    early literacy network retreat, 5
Schiller, Friedrich, 113
school, shared mission with library, 10–12
Schreiber, Becky, 94
Scotti, Tomaso, 67
self-control
    acting with, 38–39
    in young children, 37
self-reliance, 141
Senge, Peter, 91
setbacks, 4
*Seven Brides for Seven Brothers* (film), xv
*Seven Habits of Highly Effective People* (Covey), 4,
    49
Shannon, John, 94
Shauck, Stephanie, ix
ship, ix
Singer, Paula M., 95
singing, 24
Six Hats method, 91–93
*Six Thinking Hats* (De Bono), 91–92
Skokie (IL) Public Library, 75
Smirlock, Valerie, 74
Smith, Tanya Baronti, 69
social development
    in early childhood, 37
    pretend-play activities for, 39
    what Fred Rogers would do, 39–42
Society for Organizational Learning, North
    America, 91
Socrates, 10, 123
soft skills, 112
South Kingston (RI) Public Library, 24
Soviet Union, 62
Sowell, Thomas, 138
SPARK (Students Progress and Achieve with
    Reading Kits), 88

Speck, Marie, 38
Springfield-Greene County (MO) Public Library,
    24–25
Springfield-Greene County Library District,
    Missouri, 136
Squires, Barbara, 125–126
Stanton, Katie, 98
Statoil, 92
Stoltz, Dorothy, ix–x
Stoltz, Margaret, 141
Stoltz, Paul G., 168
storytime
    community benefits of collaboration, 142
    Elaine and Gilda Roadshow, 26–27
    librarian self-control and, 39
    Little Movers storytime, 83
    parent engagement with, 84
    ProjectVIEWS2, 20–21
    social/emotional development and, 74
    Wigglers Storytime, 24–25
Strand, Jessica, 10
strength
    celebrating strengths of community, 134, 136
    celebration for, 133
    core of, 122–125
    of library, identification of, 137
students, curiosity for learning, 87–89
Students Progress and Achieve with Reading Kits
    (SPARK), 88
success
    celebration, tapping spirit of, 132–134
    celebration of, 4
    library celebration to promote services,
        131–132
    questions on celebrating success, 140
    tips on celebrating/collaborating, 137–140
Suggested Reading appendix, 173–174
Sullivan, Anne, 107–108
Super Hero Collection, 123–124
Swift, Jonathan, 65
*Symphony No. 9 in D Minor* (Beethoven), 112, 113

**T**

*A Tale of a Tub* (Swift), 65
talking, 24
technology
    libraries' challenges regarding, 114
    libraries' use of for transformation, 104
    making learning fun/practical, 105–108
    media mentoring, 106–107, 108
Teichert, Tobias, 39
tenacity, 28
Tesla, Nikola, 61

thinking
    asking right questions, 91
    De Bono's six thinking hats, 91–93
    leading from any position, 94–95
    learning to think, 89
    reading great literature, 93–94
Tierney, Joyce, 116
time, 70
"To a Mouse" (Burns), 82
Tolkien, J. R. R., 31
transformation
    of Helen Keller, 107–108
    with media mentorship, 108
    technology mentoring and, 107
    transformative power of libraries, 103–104
Twain, Mark (Samuel Clemens), 167

**U**

United States, 121–122, 126
United States Constitution, 81, 85
University of Alberta Libraries, 136
University of Maryland School of Public Policy,
    171
University of Washington, 20, 21
Using Critical Incidents to Build Leadership
    Competence, 149–151

**V**

value, definition of, 37
values
    investment in, 37–38
    self-control, 38–39
Von Oech, Roger, 166

**W**

Walmart, 129
Weak, Emily, 138
weaving metaphor, 84–85
Weihenmayer, Erik, 168
A Whack on the Side of the Head: How You Can Be
    More Creative (Von Oech), 166
White, E. B., 9, 10
Whitman, Walt, 3
Wicomico County (MD) Library, 24
Wigglers Storytime, 24
Williams, Margaret, 11–12
Wilson, August, 48
Winter, Ella, 62
wisdom, Pondering Everyday Wisdom appendix,
    165–168
World War II, 121–122, 126
writing, 24

**Y**

yes, 100–102, 133
Young, Andrew, 111

**Z**

Zero to Three, ix